The Sealink Years

Miles Cowsill · John Hendy

ISBN 1 871947 35 9 (Softback)
1 871947 37 5 (Hardback)

Published by

FERRY Publications

12 Millfields Close, Kilgetty, Pembrokeshire, SA68 0SA.
Tel: 01834 813991 · Fax: 01834 814484

FOREWORD

W Gareth Cooper

With our acquisition of the Sealink business in 1990 the seal was set on the final phase of the life of one of the shipping world's most well-known brand names. As the architect of much of the major change which has taken place in the business since then I am well aware of the views of some shipping industry purists who would rather the Sealink brand had survived and that mostly everything in the company had stayed the same as it always was including the ships, the routes, the people and the style of service.

But modern business is not like that. It is driven by customer choice, quality, service and value for money and companies which do not meet the challenge of change simply fade away and die.

I'm afraid to say this could easily have been the fate of Sealink as recently as 1991.

Beset by massive overheads, old tonnage and service standards which varied wildly from route to route Sealink was, at the time, a shipping company. What we had to do was modernise the business and get our people to work to new, uniform, standards in a multi-faceted environment - in the travel industry, the leisure industry, the retailing industry, the hotel industry, the catering industry and the entertainment industry all at the same time.

The fact we operated ships as the method of generating income was, for the first time in the history of our business, recognised as merely a means to an end, a fact which may shake the shipping purists to the core.

But the results were quite startling and enabled us to strengthen our position as a dynamic force in an industry facing many challenges, not least from the Channel tunnel. Our new structure enabled us to move quickly in tactical sales and marketing initiatives which brought many benefits to us and others as markets grew. Meanwhile, our ships had become profit centres and new working practices, agreed with the co-operation of the trades unions, led us to operate in a completely new way, including live on-board working throughout our fleet.

It was inevitable, given the level of investment by Stena Line in Sealink, that, ultimately, the brand name would change once the uniformity of product offer throughout the UK and Ireland operation mirrored that of our Scandinavian parent company.

I am aware of the mixed feelings this move generated and pros and cons of such a radical change. Sealink was a powerful name and one not discarded lightly. It was a name held in great affection by those with long-standing connections with the company through its many periods of change and differing owners.

This excellent reference work charts the course of Sealink through the years. I hope you enjoy it.

W Gareth Cooper
Managing Director
Stena Line (UK) Ltd.

INTRODUCTION

To be asked to write an introduction which deals with the heyday and onwards of the British Rail Shipping & International Services Division/Sealink is indeed a great honour but at the same time a sad exercise to explain the company's ultimate transfer to others.

Although the picture I have to paint is rather bleak I must say it certainly was not always so, especially when the Labour Government stopped the Channel Tunnel workings. The exhilaration had to be experienced but unfortunately it was short-lived and the old bogey came back to haunt us.

Rest assured the S.I.S.D./Sealink showed the way and ships of the highest calibre were finally built. Safety and comfort of passengers was always paramount and with shore management co-operating with the sea staff, a most successful fleet emerged of which all participants should be justly proud.

Way back in 1945 a dynamic young manager at Dover was all for reinstating the cross Channel services. The *Canterbury* restarted the 'Golden Arrow' service and was soon replaced by the new *Invicta* while the *Autocarrier* was running cars on the Folkestone–Boulogne route. The train ferry service to Dunkerque eventually recommenced after the return of the three ships from war service and all was building towards a bright and prosperous future.

Then someone said,"What about a Channel Tunnel ?" That did it : on came the dampers, bureaucracy took over and, as the brakes were bring applied, our dynamic manager migrated to Canada. Procrastination became the order of the day and as a seafarer, like many others I was eventually destined to watch the decline and fall of the Shipping & International Services Division, later to be called Sealink (U.K.) Ltd.

In 1946, when Second Officer of the *Autocarrier*, we were talking about loading cars by ramps although it was to take another six years for this to be achieved at Dover Eastern Docks. Building a new ship in those days had to go through umpteen governmental committees before final approval and it took six years before we finally saw the delivery of the *Maid of Kent* in 1959.

The following year, as Master of the *Maid of Orleans*, one of our passengers was a prominent Greek ship-owner of the day who was off to a board meeting where the main item on the agenda was whether or not the money should be made

Captain John Arthur. (John Hendy)

available to construct a new 100,000 ton tanker. When asked how long that would take he replied, "Oh about an hour or so." There was no loss of time and money having six years of committee meetings.

The system was well and truly entrenched and as seafarers we could only watch and despair, not that we were short on comments. I recall, so well, one General Manager telling me that he had been instructed to make a case for closing the Southampton service and we all saw how quickly it was taken over by our rivals.

Having stood by the building of the m.v. *Vortigern*, I brought her out in 1969 and stayed with her for a further very happy eleven years. In March 1975 there was a 48 hour strike and I wrote to the then General Manager. The following are excerpts from that letter:

"I am writing to you as a fellow colleague of the first 'Shipping and International Services' conference held at Windsor in 1960.

It is because of our past associations and present positions that I have felt duty bound to write in an attempt to revitalise some of the fire of ambition which existed in 1960, but it is now down to a few smouldering ashes which have been further dampened by this 48 hour strike.

As recently as 1969, our then General Manager was talking to the press aboard my ship and portraying a bright and exciting future for the Shipping Division with a further twenty five *Vortigern*-type vessels to be built. Maybe that number are now in existence but most are owned by our competitors and the majority of our Sealink ships are operated by foreigners.

The reasons for these facts are not understood by Officers and Men of this section. Actions speak louder than words. The exhilaration and buoyancy you sensed at the Marine Officers' Dinner last February has subsided and morale has since sunk to a new low. Not a word has come from Management regarding proposals for the future and the closing of Heysham on top of Southampton and the hand-over of Larne and Boulogne to Townsend is seen as another nail in the coffin of the Shipping & International Services Division.

During my thirty years of service, I have seen this section bedevilled with pessimism and systematically given over to others. We could have now been running the largest, most lucrative and finest coastal shipping service in the world with the short sea routes as the jewel in the crown."

But alas, that was not to be. I retired in August 1981 when privatisation was fast approaching and during the following April, as an observer I attended a meeting when yet another General Manager introduced Mr. Sherwood of Sea Containers who was to become Sealink's new owner. Sea Containers sold to Stena and after a respectful 'wake' period the Sealink name has been dropped from the ships and correspondence and thus the final nail has been driven into the coffin of S.I.S.D. and Sealink (U.K.) Ltd.

A cruel twist of fate, but the happy memories will never be lost.

S.I.S.D./ Sealink's contribution to the Merchant Service in general and to the Ferry Service in particular will live on into the future. It showed the way on which others built.

Captain John Arthur FNI
Retired Commodore Master
Sealink (U.K.) Ltd.

The **St. Christopher** *passing the* **St. Anselm** *on Captain Arthur's last day in service - 18th August 1981. (John Hendy)*

PREFACE

The name 'Sealink' is now consigned to history, hence this present appreciation of the company, its ships and services. The British Railways shipping services were an amalgamation of fleets operated by the 'Big Four' railway companies which were nationalised in 1948. Under the initial wing of the British Transport Commission, the new regions, of which British Railways was composed, continued to build ships for the services which their predecessors had plied. This state of affairs continued until the nationalised shipping concerns were all brought under the wing of the Shipping and International Services Division (S.I.S.D.).

Hampered by a general lack of investment and controlled by managers steeped in railway bureaucracy and thinking, the railway fleet provided an adequate and reliable service during a growing period of change. On the English Channel routes, the vehicle ferry revolution saw more sailings directed towards motorists and not the connecting Boat Trains. On the Irish Sea, the long established overnight services were also ended as car ferries made their inevitable inroads into a style of traffic which had not altered for one hundred years. As the fundamental nature of the industry changed, so too did the ships that worked it.

The roll on–roll off revolution of the late 1960s made older vessels redundant and although a series of conversions extended the careers of a number of well-known ships, these were largely unsatisfactory stopgap measures until more suitable vessels entered service.

Competition from other companies highlighted B.R.'s inability to cope with the anticipated demand of the changing market and the promise of future privatisation lit the beacons of hope.

When Sealink was eventually sold for £66 million in July 1984, the deal was dubbed, "the sale of the century." The company was now owned by the Bermuda-based Sea Containers led by its entrepreneurial President, James B. Sherwood. Much was expected but Utopia was never to materialise.

Under Sea Containers' ownership however, some impressive modifications were made to the passenger accommodation of several key units within the fleet. For so long a crossing by a B.R. ferry was something to be endured

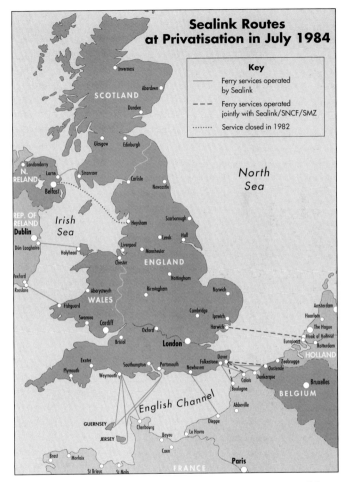

Sealink Routes at Privatisation in July 1984

rather than be enjoyed but SeaCo sought to provide a complete travel experience. This was certainly exemplified by their reintroduction of the Venice-Simplon Orient Express and the Pullman lounges on board the *Hengist* and *Horsa*.

But errors were also made and no more so than on the Channel Islands routes where costly modifications to two old ships and large fare increases heralded the 'Orient Express of the Sea'. The market was so badly misread by them that this bold initiative encouraged a cheaper rival operator to start a competing service and within months capture some 85% of the Channel Islands traffic.

The new more aggressive style of American-led management failed to cut much ice with Sealink's traditional trading partners from Holland, France and Belgium–S.M.Z., S.N.C.F. and R.M.T. The latter objected to Sealink's declared intention to raise their market share of the Ostend route from 15% to 50% and did the unthinkable by entering into a trading agreement with rivals Townsend Thoresen. With Sealink effectively shut out of Belgium, they sought to expand their operations via Dunkerque West and when a berth did eventually present itself at Zeebrugge, the ships purchased to operate the new link proved too slow to operate the required number of sailings in order to make the route pay.

The promised delivery of P&O European Ferries' 'Chunnel Beaters' in 1987 saw initial plans to stretch the *St. Anselm* and *St. Christopher* in order to match them but in the event two large, deep sea ro–ro vessels were purchased and converted at Bremerhaven. What became known as the *Fantasia* and *Fiesta* boasted a completely new concept of on-board comfort in which the interior designer attempted to create a 'floating world' by flooding the ships' accommodation with light, eye-catching signage and liner-style space and furnishings. Other operators took note and acted to follow these trend-setting ships which, at the time of entering service, were also the safest ferries afloat.

When in March 1989, the Swedish shipping company Stena Line purchased 8% of Sea Containers' shares there began the battle for the control of Sealink until the hostile take-over bid was finally completed on 31st May 1990. During SeaCo's six years, much was promised in the way of new tonnage but in the event only two car ferries and two catamarans for the Isle of Wight services were delivered.

Stena Line were no strangers to the British ferry scene and without a long series of charters and sales during the past thirty years, the industry would have been the poorer without them. If ever a vessel was required at short notice to cover a period of overhaul, breakdown or simply to provide extra capacity, it appeared that Stena was always on hand to assist.

Stena Line acquired Sealink's ferries and ports division for £259 million although Sea Containers retained the ownership of Hoverspeed, the Isle of Wight services (which they renamed Wightlink) and their share in the Isle of Man Steam Packet Company in addition to the ports of Folkestone, Newhaven and Heysham. Seafarers hoped that Stena would

Stena Sealink Line Routes December 1995

bring immediate investment into the fleet but market analysts believed that the Swedes had overstretched themselves, a fact borne out by the imposition of Operation Benchmark which was designed to save the company from financial ruin. Many cost-saving measures were introduced, the most radical being the closure of the 147 year old Folkestone–Boulogne route on the last day of 1991.

In May 1992 Stena acquired the Newhaven–Dieppe route from S.N.C.F. and reintroduced stability and growth to a service that had become the least reliable in the whole of northern Europe.

After initially operating as Sealink Stena Line and then Stena Sealink Line, on 1st January 1996 the company modified its title and became simply Stena Line. It was felt that the name 'Sealink' still carried overtones of the old 'railway boats' image, of rather functional and somewhat austere interiors which so marked much of the fleet until the mid-1980s.

Since the demise of the nationalised operation in 1984, new tonnage has appeared on all routes. This has been acquired from Scandinavian operators and is therefore shallow drafted, lacking in essential lorry carrying capacity and boasts the 'glitzy' accommodation so typical of the Nordic cruise-ferry concept. It is sobering to realise that no large purpose-built ferries were constructed for Sealink following the introduction of the four 'Saint' class ships in 1980/81.

In this respect Sealink singularly failed to compete with its competitors all of whom have strengthened their operations and fleets during these intervening years.

When nationalisation in 1948 brought the railway under public ownership, the vast majority of the travelling public used the services then provided. Without any significant competition, the trains and ships of British Railways were mass people movers–'Joe Public' knew little else and travelled from the same ports on the same routes in ships bearing local names with which he could associate. B.R. was the people's carrier and this concept stood the company well for many years. Even today, in an age of increasing uniformity, the burger bar image with catering assistants dressed in shirts and braces and the belief that customers are there to be entertained, reinforces the slick 'down town' expectations of the mass market.

So what was special about Sealink? Firstly the name was a household word–a marketing man's dream–leading all who heard it straight to the core of the company's business. Secondly, the company was well-known for operating traditional ships on traditional routes with long historic associations. Thirdly, the company operated a fleet of widely

The **Duke of Lancaster** *seen leaving Heysham. (D.I. Harmsworth)*

differing ships, most of which boasted interesting backgrounds and each of which had its own air of individuality. Fourthly, those who worked for Sealink were conscious of the long tradition of British seafaring to which they belonged. Fifthly, most who knew the company admired the way in which it was successful in spite of severe financial restraints which prevented the introduction of, often necessary, new tonnage in the face of increased competition. Sixthly, these financial constraints, added to the dyed-in-the-wool attitude of some senior railway management, meant that the fleet was slow to change and therefore often anachronistic. Seventhly, there was the association with other fleets and routes operated by the Dutch, Belgian and French partners forming the Sealink consortium. Eighthly, Sealink was served by an excellent public relations department which promoted the fleet particularly through such excellent journals as 'Sealink News.'

Throughout the twenty five years covered by this present publication, the writers can claim to have sailed on most of the ships in the Sealink fleet and during this period they became great admirers of the company, its vessels and those who operated them. Many friends have been made along the way and it is hoped that this publication should serve as a tribute both to them and to the fine company which they represented.

Bibliography

Sealink Dover–Calais
Ferries of Dover
Folkestone–Boulogne
Wightlink
Newhaven–Dieppe–the Car Ferry era
Harwich–Hook of Holland - A 100 Years of Service
Sealink British Ferries to Ireland
Fishguard-Rosslare
British Nationalised Shipping (Clegg & Styring)
Channel Islands Railway Steamers (Le Scelleur)
Designing Ships for Sealink (Ripley & Rogan)
Lymington–Sound of Success (Brown)
Cruising Monthly
British Ferry Scene
Sea Breezes

The **Avalon** on the buoys off Parkeston Quay in August 1974. (Ferry Publications Library)

Acknowledgements

The writers express their sincere thanks to Captain John Arthur for agreeing to write the Introduction. Thanks must also go to the following: Chris Laming (Public Relations Manager, Stena Line), Phil Neuman (FotoFlite), Alex Whomes (White Horse Ferries), Jim Ashby, John May, Andy Jones, Michael Connellan (Stena Line) and Pat Somner of Ferry Publications.

Ferry Publications acknowledge their grateful thanks to Stena Line (U.K.) Ltd. for agreeing to sponsor this publication.

Further Reading

DESIGNING SHIPS FOR SEALINK
by Don Ripley & Tony Rogan.

The companion volume to this book was published earlier this year. Written by Sealink's former principal naval architect and his deputy, the unique inside story is given behind the construction of many of the ships involved in 'The Sealink Years.' Available from Ferry Publications. Price £10.30, including p&p within the UK.

THE SEALINK YEARS

At a press conference during early November 1969, it was announced that British Rail's Shipping & International Services Division (S.I.S.D.) had adopted a new brand name–Sealink. Among other names considered were Sea Rail, Inter Marine, Sea Vector and Eurolink. It is of interest that twenty five years later, at the time when Sealink's then Swedish owners were considering abandoning the famous, household name, a new company adopted the name Eurolink with which to commence a service across the southern North Sea.

Mr. J. L. Harrington became Deputy Chairman of the S.I.S.D. as from 1st January 1970 and was quick to define the division's move to a fleet of two types of vessel. Their future policy was to gain year-round utilisation of vessels and so container ships and multi-purpose passenger ferries, similar to the new *Vortigern*, would be built. He stated, "New routes are constantly under study and every effort is being made to maintain and improve the company as the largest short-sea ferry operator in the world."

Cross Channel & Irish Sea

◆ 1970

Harwich: British Rail's last passenger ferry *Avalon* operated her usual spring and autumn cruises: from Harwich to Copenhagen, Stockholm, Leningrad and Bornholm from 28th May until 10th June and from Harwich to Corunna, Gibraltar, Casablanca and Vigo between 17th–30th September. Fares were from £75 and £220.

The mainstays of the Anglo-Dutch Harwich–Hook of Holland ferry service were B.R.'s *St. George* (sailing by day from Harwich) running opposite the S.M.Z. (Zeeland Steamship Company) ferry *Koningin Juliana* which ran the day sailing from the Hook. The passenger vessels *Avalon* and the Dutch *Koningin Wilhelmina* provided relief services every night between 18th June and 6th September.

During the first six months of 1970, carryings rose by 20% on the route–49,000 motorists and 25,000 cars.

The **St. David** seen at Heysham at the end of her career. (D.I. Harmsworth)

Dover: Until 1970, British Rail's pool partners French National Railways (S.N.C.F.) had operated their twin car ferries *Compiegne* (1958) and *Chantilly* (1966) on the Calais–Dover service while B.R. operated the turbine steamers *Lord Warden* (1952), *Maid of Kent* (1959), *Normannia* (1952 but converted to a car ferry in 1964) and *Dover* (1965) on the premier link to Boulogne.

Increasing competition from both Townsend Thoresen and Swedish hovercraft operators Hoverlloyd at Calais coupled with a desire not to compete with the B.R. hovercraft subsidiary Seaspeed on the Boulogne route saw an inevitable change of emphasis for the 1970 season.

The two French ferries increased daily sailings from one to three during March (two months earlier than in 1969) and were to offer 64 sailings each week in the peak period as opposed to just 38 in the previous year. Sailings to Boulogne were reduced from 78 to 66 during the same period and the B.R. car ferry *Lord Warden* was rostered to operate to Calais. The 'Warden' seriously damaged her starboard side while berthing at Calais on 2nd August and with a spare propeller and propeller shaft, she sailed to Harland & Wolff's yard in the Royal Albert Dock (London) for repair. Three days later the *Maid of Kent* damaged her stern at Dover Eastern Docks and retired to Rotterdam for repairs, during which time the *Normannia* took up her roster.

The 'Golden Arrow' passenger steamer *Invicta* was unusually chartered for an Ostend sailing on 23rd May. The Folkestone vessel *Maid of Orleans* worked her 'Arrow' sailings from Dover to Calais on that day.

Folkestone: Plans to build a new £750,000 car ferry terminal and twin car ferries for Folkestone were unveiled in the spring and were later approved by the Government. The Folkestone–Boulogne service became one class as from 31st May. Some 860,000 passengers passed through the port during the first nine months of the year–an increase of 50,000 on 1969.

Channel Islands: On 8th May the passenger steamer *St. Patrick* left Folkestone for Guernsey and Jersey to undertake a series of excursions to St. Malo before returning to Dover on 11th May. The Dieppe car ferry *Villandry* was scheduled to operate sailings from Le Havre and Cherbourg to Jersey over the Whitsun weekend.

The Channel Islands cargo vessel *Winchester* was finally withdrawn from service at the completion of her Guernsey–Weymouth sailing on 29th December. Renamed *Exeter,* and having been sold to Chandris Cruises, she arrived at Piraeus on 24th May 1971. Later converted to a cruise ship and renamed *Radiosa* the vessel was broken up in Greece during 1995.

Fishguard: Side loading car ferry operations between the Welsh port and Rosslare had seen a 6% rise in 1969 with as many as 60,000 vehicles carried in the converted *St. David* and *Duke of Rothesay,* which had herself been converted, and subsequently transferred from Heysham, in early 1967. Daily capacity was for 474 cars and 5,600 passengers.

Holyhead: The *Holyhead Ferry I* and half-sister *Dover* were engaged in a two ship seasonal car ferry working between 22nd May and 19th September. The mainstays of the route were still the 1949-built, overnight passenger vessels *Cambria* and *Hibernia*.

On 23rd May, fire seriously damaged the 120 year old Britannia Tubular Bridge across the Menai Strait thereby isolating the port of Holyhead from all rail connections. The car ferry service continued but the passenger vessels, along with the rail connected cargo boat operations, were switched to Heysham from where the Dun Laoghaire service operated until the bridge was eventually repaired. A third passenger vessel was required at weekends and this role was filled by the Fishguard steamer *St. David*. B.R. chartered Fisher's *Kingsnorth Fisher* to operate three sailings from Holyhead to Barrow during mid-June to retrieve their eleven trapped locomotives from the Anglesey port.

Heysham: A new 6 hour 50 minute link from Dun Laoghaire to Heysham operated three times each week between 27th June–19th September using the Holyhead car ferries *Holyhead Ferry I* and *Dover*.

From 28th December 1969, services on the Belfast route became one class only on the overnight service. Preparations were underway for a total restructuring of the Belfast link with the introduction of drive-on daylight crossings. The *Duke of Lancaster* made her last passenger sailing from Heysham to Belfast on 3rd January after which she entered Harland & Wolff's yard for conversion and the *Cambria* was switched to operate the link. The *Caledonian Princess* (from Stranraer) moved to Heysham, vice the *Cambria*, in the following month. The 'Argyll' (the first to be converted) restarted with the 23.40 from Heysham on 24th February.

The converted vessels had a vehicle deck headroom of 6' 6", one class cabin accommodation for 400 and indoor seating for 550, while passenger certificates were reduced from 1,800 to 1,200. The 'Lancaster' arrived back on station, releasing the *Duke of Rothesay*, on 25th April. The new 'Daylight Service' was officially inaugurated by Princess Alexandra on 25th May.

The *Cambria* arrived at Cammell Laird's Birkenhead yard on 18th August after heavily damaging her bow at Heysham in bad weather. The stand-by vessel *St. David* was on hand until released by the *Cambria* on 23rd September.

The *St. David* was now advertised for sale with delivery at Heysham. Unfortunately her would-be purchasers defaulted and she was again offered for sale with all bids due in by 4th December. The vessel was eventually purchased by Chandris Cruises and, renamed *Holyhead*, sailed from that port to Perama (Greece) on 17th January 1971.

Stranraer: The chartered Swedish ferry *Stena Nordica* was sub-chartered to Burns Laird and operated, vice the *Lion*, on the Belfast–Ardrossan link during early October.

The 'Nordica's' eventual replacement, the new *Ailsa Princess,* was launched at Cantiere Navale, Breda, Venice on 28th November. A new £120,000 ramp was ordered at Stranraer to replace the original 1939 linkspan.

◆ 1971

Harwich: The *Avalon's* 1971 spring cruise, between 8th–21st May, was from Harwich to Bergen, Narvik, Trondheim and Stavanger whilst the autumn cruise (18th September–1st October) was to Lisbon, Tangier, Vigo and St. Nazaire.

Dover: The new *Vortigern* was chartered for the 20th International Railway Congress and sailed from Southend Pier to Greenwich on 22nd May.

Folkestone: At the end of the summer season (25th September) the *St. Patrick*, which had operated in the Dover Strait since Christmas 1964, operated her final scheduled crossing to Boulogne although a "special" was given on the following day. She sailed to lay-up at Newhaven.

Newhaven: The *Dover* was in collision with the West Pier at Newhaven on 23rd October and damaged her starboard propeller. She was sent to Southampton for repairs.

Above: The **Maid of Orleans** *(right) and the R.M.T. vessel* **Reine Astrid** *at Dover's Admiralty Pier in 1975. (John Hendy)*

Channel Islands: The former Associated Humber Line's (A.H.L.) cargo vessel *Selby* (sold October 1972) was aground in gales at Jersey during January. The Southampton–Channel Islands vessel was towed to Marchwood by the Newhaven tug *Meeching* and Commodore Shipping's *Carsten* (normally Portsmouth–Channel Islands) was chartered.

The **Ailsa Princess** *seen at Venice on sea trials. (Tony Rogan)*

The *St. Patrick* made a welcome return to the Islands when she operated a series of five sailings from Jersey to St. Malo. The steamer left Dover for St. Helier on 30th April and finished at St. Malo on 8th May.

Plans to replace the cargo ships *Elk* and *Moose* were announced. Two new ships (*Jersey Fisher* and *Guernsey Fisher*), owned by James Fisher & Sons Ltd., would operate to the Islands from Portsmouth, thereby ending the railway shipping connection with Southampton.

Fishguard: The *Duke of Rothesay* was booked to operate two Cardigan Bay cruises on 11th April and 12th September. Plans were in hand to invest some £600,000 to convert the Fishguard–Rosslare route from side to stern loading. The late arrival of the new Stranraer ship meant that the *Holyhead Ferry I* was retained at Fishguard during the early part of the year as the *Caledonian Princess* was in service on the North Channel.

Heysham: The *Holyhead Ferry I* and the *Hibernia* were relieving on the Dun Laoghaire mail service during early spring. The new Dun Laoghaire–Heysham service was axed at the end of the 1971 season (18th September) so that the *Holyhead Ferry I* and *Dover* could concentrate on the central corridor route.

The German vessels, *Saaletal* and *Donautal*, on charter to Coast Lines, started a joint Belfast Steam Ship/ B.R. cargo service to Belfast. The first ship commenced operations on 1st November.

Meanwhile the former A.H.L. cargo ships *Darlington* and *Harrogate* were withdrawn from service.

Stranraer: The port's new linkspan was installed on 16th March, but following a mechanical error, sank a week later. The chartered *Stena Nordica* operated from Ardrossan until the linkspan was repositioned. The ship finally finished on 27th March after which she was returned to Sweden (she had started her B.R. charter in February 1966). The A.S.N. ro-ro ferry *Baltic Ferry* was briefly chartered before another Stena charter was taken, this time on the *Stena Trailer*. Renamed *Dalriada*, the vessel entered service on 24th June.

The new *Ailsa Princess* finally entered service with the 07.00 from Stranraer on 7th July. She was off service two days later with engine problems and required minor bow-door modifications. Her registered owners were Carpass (Shipping) Co. Ltd., a London company jointly owned by the British Railways Board and Great Universal Stores. The ship was operated on a lease-back scheme for tax advantages and was duly registered in London rather than Stranraer.

◆ **1972**

Harwich: Government approval for a second vehicle ferry for the Harwich–Hook route meant that the *Avalon's* days were now numbered. On 28th April she was chartered for a long weekend to Emden and advertised cruises were: 'the Viking cruise' between 6th–17th May during which time she visited Visby (Gotland), Copenhagen and Oslo whilst between 16th–29th September 'the Fiesta cruise' sailed via Dover to Bordeaux, Seville, Gibraltar and Santander.

During the early part of the year, the train ferries *Cambridge Ferry* and *Essex Ferry* undertook ten very unusual sailings from Harwich to Dublin's North Wall with rolling stock for C.I.E.

The new £750,000 Parkeston Quay passenger terminal was opened on 12th September. Meanwhile the Rotterdam cargo service finished on 1st September thereby releasing the *Colchester* (built 1959 but converted to carry larger containers in 1968). Dutch partners S.M.Z. continued the service with chartered tonnage.

Dover: The car ferry *Lord Warden* was unusually engaged on the famous "Golden Arrow" Dover–Calais passenger service between 2nd–20th February. The *Invicta* (Captain Elgar Blaxland) ended her career on 8th August operating her usual 12.25 from Dover Admiralty Pier and 16.05 return from Calais Maritime. Built at Denny's in 1940, the steamer had maintained the "Golden Arrow" link for 26 years and was the only Dover Strait turbine to serve on the route for which she was created throughout her career. She sailed to Newhaven to lay-up two days later although plans for the *St. Patrick's* new owners to purchase the veteran steamer had fallen-through.

The *Maid of Orleans* finished with the 17.00 Boulogne–Folkestone on 7th August before sailing to Dover ready to take up the *Invicta's* schedules on 9th August. Thereafter she operated the legendary service until its demise on 30th September. The following day, at the start of the

*In 1976 the **Holyhead Ferry I** was converted to drive-through operations by Swan Hunter. She emerged as the **Earl Leofric** and is seen approaching the Kent coast on an afternoon sailing from Calais. (FotoFlite)*

*The **Shepperton Ferry** leaving Dover in 1972. (John Hendy)*

winter timetable, the service became one class and the former passenger ship sailings were incorporated into the new *Hengist* and *Horsa's* rosters.

The train ferry *Shepperton Ferry* completed her service on 26th August after which she retired to the Wellington Dock to await disposal. The B.R.B. purchased the *Anderida* from Stena Line off the stocks at Brevik and the vessel left Kristiansand on 22nd August arriving at Dover two days later via Dunkerque. The 1,601 gross tons ship entered the train ferry service on 28th August. Her registered owners were Carpass (Shipping) Co. Ltd.

The *Shepperton Ferry* was towed for scrapping at Bilbao by the tug *Fairplay XI* on 12th September. Meanwhile the *Invicta* left for scrap in Holland on 21st September behind the tug *Michel Petersen*.

Folkestone: The *Hengist* and *Horsa* were officially named at Brest on 29th April. Delays in the completion of the new car ferry terminal meant that the official opening was delayed from 1st June until 1st July.

The passenger steamer *Maid of Orleans* departed for Jersey on 20th July to cover for the *Caesarea*, resuming in the Dover Strait two days later. Her roster was covered by the S.N.C.F. passenger steamer *Cote d'Azur* which eventually finished service with her usual 17.25 Folkestone–Calais on 30th September. Renamed *Azur*, the vessel was sold to Monaco but saw no further service.

The *Hengist* (Captain Ernest Bussey) was delivered on 6th June and called at Newhaven for berthing trials on the following day. Her inaugural crossing was on 16th June when she operated from Folkestone to Boulogne and Calais. The ship entered service on 19th June (vice the *Maid of Kent*) as a passenger-only vessel. Her owners were "Sealink Ltd"– a wholly-owned subsidiary of the B.R.B. - but she was later transferred to the ownership of Carpass (Shipping) Co. Ltd. The *Hengist* commenced car ferry operations from Folkestone on 1st July and for the first time included an overnight call at Ostend following B.R.'s gaining of a 15% share in the Belgian link. Her schedules were as follows: 04.05 from Ostend, 10.50 Folkestone, 13.50 Boulogne, 17.00 Folkestone, 19.50 Boulogne, 22.45 Folkestone to Ostend.

Sistership *Horsa* (Captain Godfrey Barron) arrived on 30th July and was hastily called into service vice the *Vortigern* on the 07.30 from Dover to Boulogne on 2nd August. She remained on this roster for three days before taking over from the *Maid of Orleans* at Folkestone on 8th August. She commenced her multi-purpose mode on 19th August

*A view of **Lord Warden** in dry dock at Southampton. (Ferry Publications Library)*

*The **Hengist** at Folkestone on the opening day of the car ferry service in July 1972. (John Hendy)*

operating: 01.45 from Ostend, 07.00 Folkestone, 10.05 Calais, 13.20 Folkestone, 17.00 Boulogne, 20.15 to Ostend.

Interestingly the new ships were built with half an eye on their eventual transfer to the Heysham–Belfast service should the Channel Tunnel be built. Their upper vehicle decks would have been converted into cabins for the longer service and the stern docking bridges were required to go astern up the Lagan.

From a visual point of view, the twins were the first ships to carry the word "Sealink" along their hulls. This practice was adopted by the rest of the fleet in the following year.

Newhaven: The passenger steamer *St. Patrick* was sold for a reported £42,000 to the Greek company, S. Geriasimos Phetouris and renamed *Thermopolae*, she departed for Piraeus on 9th March arriving there on 28th March.

The *Caledonian Princess* was on the Dieppe crossing between 11th May and 20th June after which she sailed to Fishguard.

A new Norwegian-built ro-ro ship, the *Capitaine Le Goff*, eventually entered service for S.N.C.F. on 8th August. The ship was formerly the *Admiral Carrier I* and had been delayed from entering service while stern modifications were made.

Newhaven's £250,000 passenger terminal was opened on 31st May. It replaced the 92 year old London Brighton & South Coast Railway station building which was demolished.

At Brest, the new *Senlac* was floated out of the dry dock in which she was built on 1st December.

Channel Islands: The cargo ships *Elk* and *Moose* were retired from service in October 1972, the *Elk* operating the final sailing from Southampton on 29th September, while the *Moose* was retained to carry cars from Weymouth. Both ships were sold to the Valmas Shipping Co. (Greece) and underwent several changes of name before the *Nasim* (ex.*Elk*) was lost in February 1976. The *Agios Dionyssios* I (ex. *Moose*) was reported sold at the end of 1995.

The seven year charter of the *Lune Fisher* ended in January 1972 while the new *Guernsey Fisher* and *Jersey Fisher* entered service on 6th January and 20th February respectively. They remained in service until 27th October and 29th September 1977.

The *Caesarea* was damaged at St. Peter Port in fog on 19th July and later sailed to Falmouth for repairs. The *Maid of Orleans* sailed directly to Jersey from Folkestone arriving there at 10.15 on 20th April. Thereafter she offered a round sailing to Weymouth but as she was required back at Folkestone for the weekend, sailed from Jersey and Guernsey to Newhaven where she disembarked her passengers.

Fishguard: The *Duke of Rothesay* was scheduled to operate two Cardigan Bay cruises during the year. The first was on Easter Sunday (2nd April) when 316 passengers enjoyed a six hour cruise towards Aberystwyth while the second was on 14th September. The ship was fitted with stern doors during her refit at Holyhead.

Poor bookings meant that only one car ferry was required at Fishguard during 1972. The new linkspan was officially opened at the port on 6th July by the B.R.B. Chairman, the Rt. Hon. Richard Marsh. The *Caledonian Princess* operated the new-look service allowing the *Duke of Rothesay* to sail to lay-up.

Holyhead: The Britannia Railway Bridge across the Menai Strait was reopened on 30th January. The traditional mail boat service was therefore transferred from its temporary home at Heysham and with the *Hibernia* on overhaul at the time, it was left to the *Cambria* (20.45 from Dun Laoghaire) and the *Holyhead Ferry I* to recommence operations at Holyhead. The 'HF I' sailed 'light' to Holyhead

Right: *The **Falaise** bow-in at St. Peter Port, Guernsey, after her transfer to the Channel Islands service in 1973. (Ferry Publications Library)*

Bottom Left: *The **Normannia** beached in the Tidal Basin at Dover's Western Docks after holing herself in July 1974. (Andrew Jones)*

Bottom right: *The Dunkerque train ferry **Shepperton Ferry** in the Wellington Dock at Dover after her withdrawal from service in August 1972. (John Hendy)*

Above: *The post-1964 Sealink funnel colours as worn by the* **Sarnia**. *(Jim Ashby)*

Top right: *The famous Tony Rogan funnel design which was a feature of all major Sealink vessels built during the 1970s. It is seen here to full advantage on the* **Hengist**. *(John May)*

Bottom right: *Keeping her clean - painters over the side of the* **St. Christopher**. *(Jim Ashby)*

from Heysham to take up the 03.15 on 31st January.

With the *Duke of Rothesay* not required at Fishguard for the summer, she became the second car ferry at Holyhead thereby allowing the *Lord Warden* to lay-by for the season at Newhaven.

The cargo steamers *Slieve Bawn* and *Slieve Bearnagh* left Holyhead for scrapping in Spain on 15th June. The *Colchester* was on the Holyhead–Dublin container service at this time while the *Brian Boroime* and *Rhodri Mawr* were engaged on the Belfast container link.

◆ 1973

Harwich: The *Norfolk Ferry* and *Essex Ferry* both had their sterns modified so that they could fit the Dunkerque rail linkspan.

The new Hook of Holland vehicle ferry *St. Edmund* was named at Cammell Laird's Birkenhead yard on 13th November but, due to strong winds, she was not launched until the following day.

Dover: The *Normannia* was sold to S.N.C.F. for the summer period for a sum equal to the charter fee for one season. She was registered in Calais and provided a link between the withdrawal of the passenger steamer *Cote d'Azur* and the pending entry into service of the *Chartres* in 1974. The *Chartres* was launched at Nantes on 12th September.

The *Maid of Kent* (1959) collided with the quay at Boulogne on 10th September and was towed to Dunkerque for remedial repairs before she sailed to Holyhead to be prepared for the new Weymouth-Cherbourg link in 1974.

Folkestone: Due to the inability of the *Hengist* and *Horsa* to maintain their advertised schedules, sailings between Folkestone and Boulogne were retimed at 100 minutes.

Newhaven: The *Senlac* was officially named at Brest on 3rd March and arrived at Newhaven on 5th April. The vessel entered service with the 11.45 to Dieppe on 2nd May.

Channel Islands: The *Holyhead Ferry I* left Dover for Fishguard on 11th March but was diverted to Weymouth to deputise for the *Caesarea* which had damaged fuel tanks

The cargo vessel **Slieve Donard** *seen leaving Heysham.*
(D.I. Harmsworth)

when grounding at St. Helier on the night of the 7th–8th March. The 'HF I' sailed to Guernsey and arrived back at Weymouth on 12th March, it being stated that she was too large to fit St. Helier Harbour at Jersey.

Replaced in service by the *Senlac*, the Newhaven car ferry *Falaise* was earmarked to open a new car ferry service to Jersey and on 21st April she arrived at Weymouth to test the linkspan. A trial run to Jersey was carried out four days later before the new service commenced on 1st June. Meanwhile the States of Guernsey announced that they were to spend £175,000 on a new linkspan to enable a vehicle ferry operation from there in 1974. The *Normannia* was chartered for a St. Malo–Jersey excursion on 28th April and, after her season at Dover, sailed to Weymouth taking up the Channel Islands car ferry service from the *Falaise* on 13th December.

Fishguard: The ro-ro freight vessel *Neckartal* was chartered for the Rosslare service before sailing to Stranraer late in the year.

Holyhead: The *Duke of Rothesay* opened the seasonal Dun Laoghaire car ferry service on 17th April between the overnight 'mail' runs.

Heysham: First class travel was unexpectedly reintroduced on 31st December 1972. A programme of Solway Firth cruises was drawn up for operation on summer Sundays and Tuesdays.

◆ **1974**

Harwich: Early in the year it was announced that the new Hook car ferry *St. Edmund* would enter service on 1st July, replacing the *Avalon* which would be converted to a car ferry for the Fishguard-Rosslare route, thus allowing the *Caledonian Princess* to transfer to the Channel Islands.

The *Avalon's* final advertised crossings were from Harwich on 30th August returning the following night although Christmas reliefs were given on 20th and 21st December. The ship finally left Harwich on 29th December sailing to Swan Hunter at South Shields for conversion to a car ferry. She had sailed 383,000 miles on the Hook route in addition to a further 56,000 miles on her popular cruises.

The *St. Edmund* eventually carried out speed trials over the measured mile on 13th December and arrived at Harwich on Christmas Eve.

Dover: The new S.N.C.F. multi-purpose vessel *Chartres* carried out berthing trials at Dover on 18th February and commenced service on 25th February on unadvertised freight runs to Dunkerque. A manning dispute saw the ship blocking the Dunkerque rail linkspan between 12th–18th March and the 'Night Ferry' (London–Paris/ Brussels sleeper) passengers were diverted via Calais in the *Vortigern*.

The final pre-war train ferry, A.L.A's *Twickenham Ferry* was finally withdrawn from service on 24th May. Her last sailing had been at 17.30 (retimed at 18.20) on 5th May but serious boiler defects saw the steamer towed to Santander for scrapping.

The *Maid of Orleans'* second visit to Weymouth saw the *Duke of Rothesay* on the Dover–Calais passenger service on 28th June. This was the only time that one of the former Heysham 'Dukes' ever operated in the English Channel.

The withdrawal of the 'Le Twick' and the continued delay of the entry into service of the *Saint Eloi* (due in service in 1972 but seized by her yard's creditors at Genoa) called for remedial measures. The S.N.C.F. ro-ro ferry *Transcontainer I* (Dunkerque–Felixstowe service) had rail lines fitted and

carried out berthing trials at Dover on 24th October, replacing the *Anderida* during her overhaul period from 10th November.

Weymouth: The *Maid of Kent* commenced the new Cherbourg link on 6th April operating throughout the season until 12th October at 09.45 from Weymouth with a 15.00 return. Turbine troubles on 8th April saw the ship off service until 30th May.

The *Maid of Orleans* paid a second visit to the islands arriving at Weymouth on 28th June vice the *Sarnia* which was off service with turbine troubles. The 'Maid' returned to the Dover Strait on 8th July.

Following her boiler failure, the *Falaise* was prematurely withdrawn from service on 14th August. Cars were carried by cargo vessels until the Swedish car ferry *Svea Drott* (1966) took over on 19th August. She remained in service until 26th September requiring to berth at Southampton on 8th September when gales closed Weymouth. The *Caledonian Princess* then took up the service until the *Normannia* arrived for the winter on 26th October.

The *Svea Drott* was eventually purchased to replace the *Caesarea* in the Weymouth-based fleet.

The *Falaise* was towed from Holyhead to breakers in Bilbao on 31st December.

Fishguard: The ro-ro vessel *Preseli* (ex. *Isartal*) was chartered for two years and commenced service to Rosslare on 26th April. Passenger services were extended by 15 minutes during the spring in order to conserve fuel. Similar measures were taken at Holyhead and Heysham. The *Caledonian Princess* and the *Duke of Rothesay* exchanged rosters during mid- August thereby seeing the 'Duke' back at Fishguard while the 'Caley P' worked from Holyhead.

Holyhead: It was announced that a new £650,000 linkspan would be built in the Inner Harbour at Holyhead thereby allowing both rail and vehicle traffic to use the same vessel at off-peak periods.

Heysham: On 24th July, it was announced that the Heysham–Belfast passenger and vehicle service would be withdrawn on 27th October. The route, opened by the Midland Railway in 1904, was suffering annual losses of over

*The **Vortigern** newly arrived at Dover Admiralty Pier from her builders in July 1969 with the 'Golden Arrow' steamer **Invicta** astern. Dover Marine station is on the left while the train ferry **Twickenham Ferry** sits in the ferry dock. (Ferry Publications Library)*

*The **Antrim Princess** leaving Stranraer (Ferry Publications Library)*

£500,000. The closure date was later put back to 5th April 1975.

Stranraer: The ro-ro vessel *Stena Carrier* was purchased by the B.R.B. and on 7th July arrived in the Wellington Dock at Dover for remedial work. She was renamed *Ulidia* before proceeding to Middlesbrough for dry-docking during late August. The ship entered service in December.

Damage to the Stranraer linkspan saw all vehicle traffic switched to Ardrossan between 4th–9th December.

◆ 1975

Harwich: The *St. Edmund* finally entered service between Harwich and the Hook on 19th January. Accommodation was for some 1,400 passengers (1,000 by night) and 296 cars.

The cargo vessel *Colchester* was sold during the year to Cypriot owners and renamed *Taurus II*. Towards the end of her career she served on a number of routes including Holyhead–Dublin and Heysham–Belfast. She enjoyed brief charter periods to McAndrew's and James Fisher & Sons. While working in the latter's employ, the ship had an engine room fire during routine bunkering in Rotterdam. After repairs at Parkeston Quay she sailed to Holyhead for lay-up pending sale. Subsequent names were: *Gloriana* (1979), *Sea Wave* (1984), *Taurus* (1985) and *Diana* (1991).

The container ship *Isle of Ely* made her final Sealink voyages during November. Since 1972, she had led a rather peripatetic career seeing service on Heysham–Belfast, Southampton–Channel Islands and Fishguard–Waterford before finishing with a brief spell on Harwich–Dunkerque. During November she was laid-up at Barrow before being sold and renamed *Spice Island* (1978) and later *Spice Island Girl* (1979). In September 1984 she was sold for scrapping at Bruges.

Dover: The new A.L.A. train ferry *Saint Eloi* carried out berthing trials at Dover on 25th February and commenced service on 1st March.

The passenger steamer *Maid of Orleans* (Captain George Sutcliffe) completed her final crossing from Calais on 27th September although a 'special' from Boulogne was operated the next day. She sailed for lay-up at Newhaven on 30th

*The **St. Edmund** entered service on 19th January 1975. (FotoFlite)*

September and was towed by the tug *Ibaizabel Tres* for breaking in Spain on 6th November. Her sailings would be covered by the *Caesarea* in 1976.

The *Senlac* was switched from Newhaven to Dover where she operated vice her sister ship *Hengist* from Dover–Boulogne–Folkestone–Boulogne–Dover from 31st December until 14th January 1976.

Folkestone: The *Lord Warden* arrived to cover overhauls on 6th January which included an overnight freight run to Ostend in her schedules. The 'Warden's' facility to carry just one lorry meant that she was backed-up by the *Anderida*. Gales on 20th January saw the *Horsa* blown onto the *Lord Warden* at Folkestone bringing to a close one of the strangest pieces of B.R. re-rostering.

Towards the close of the year, the *Valencay* arrived at Calais on 26th November and took over the Folkestone route until 19th January 1976.

Newhaven: The *Lord Warden* worked the Dieppe route during two weekends in June vice the *Villandry*.

Channel Islands: With the *Earl Godwin* (ex. *Svea Drott*) late in entering service, the *Caledonian Princess* operated the car ferry service from July. The *Sarnia* experienced more turbine troubles and was off service between 29th April and 15th May. Meanwhile sistership *Caesarea* served her last full season on the route before finishing with the 08.15 from Jersey on 6th October.

Fishguard: The converted *Avalon* entered service to Rosslare on 18th July. The £1.75 million reconstruction provided space for 1,200 passengers and 200 cars. The *Duke of Lancaster* had operated the link since early July to allow the *Caledonian Princess* to transfer to the Channel Islands routes.

Holyhead: Following the arrival of the *Avalon* at Fishguard in mid-July, the *Duke of Lancaster* switched to Holyhead where she operated the summer service with the *Dover*. Coupled with the closure of Heysham, sisterships *Duke of Rothesay* and the *Duke of Argyll* were now surplus to requirements and were offered for sale.

Meanwhile a new car ferry was being built at Aalborg in Denmark and the *Cambria* was withdrawn from service on 7th September, following the 20.45 from Dun Laoghaire and after which the time-honoured sleeping on-board facilities were withdrawn, other than when the ship was at sea on a scheduled crossing. The ship arrived at Barrow for lay-up on 31st October.

The *Hibernia* completed her season on 5th October. The following day, the traditional 'mailboat' sailings (03.15 from Holyhead and 20.45 from Dun Laoghaire) were taken over by a car ferry on a single vessel working.

The *Duke of Rothesay* was sold for scrapping at Faslane where she arrived, via Greenock, on 18th October while the 'Argyll' was sold to Cynthia Navigation Ltd. and left Barrow as the *Neptunia* on 19th October. She arrived at Piraeus on 31st October.

On 30th November, the Dublin livestock and general cargo service duly closed after which the *Isle of Ely* sailed to Barrow for lay-up.

*The **St. George** leaving Harwich. (Ferry Publications Library)*

Heysham: Closure of the Belfast route duly occurred on 5th April with the *Duke of Argyll* making the final sailing to Ulster and the *Duke of Lancaster* the last crossing to Heysham. The vessels were sent to lay up at Barrow.

Stranraer: The *Maid of Kent* covered the winter refit period of the *Ailsa Princess* between 31st March and 26th April.

◆ **1976**

Harwich: Unusually the spare *Maid of Kent* was switched to the Harwich-Zeebrugge route during January where she shipped trade cars for a period of about two weeks.

Dover: The *Caesarea* returned from dry-docking at Calais on 13th April and took up seasonal service operating agents' specials mainly from Folkestone.

With ever-increasing degrees of roll on traffic wishing to cross the Dover Strait, the *Holyhead Ferry I* was sent to Swan Hunter's to be converted to drive-through operations. The £1.85 million work took longer than expected and so the

LIFE-RAFT STATION F

LIFE-RAFT STATION D

*On the promenade deck of the car ferry **Maid of Kent**. Her ample deck space was made possible by raising her lifeboats thereby giving passengers uninterrupted views of the Channel. Teak decks were also a feature of this classic Denny-built vessel. (Jim Ashby)*

spare Belgian car ferry *Artevelde* was chartered to operate her Dover–Calais roster from 30th June until 25th September. With the 'HF I' being renamed *Earl Leofric*, she arrived at Dover on 23rd September and took up sailings two days later. Car capacity was increased to 205 units but her passenger accommodation was reduced to 725.

The *Dover* (to be renamed *Earl Siward*) was sent to Aalborg for similar drive-through conversion to the *Earl Leofric*. The ship was due back with the 19.50 from Dover to Calais on 1st July 1977.

The new port at Dunkerque West was opened on 5th July and all train ferry services were switched there from the old tidal port in the city to the east. Crossings were reduced from 3 hours 45 minutes to 2 hours 20 minutes and Sealink attempted to generate an Eastern Docks ro-ro service using initially the *Normannia* and latterly the *Compiegne*. Neither ship was satisfactory and the new initiative was unsuccessful.

Channel Islands: The much-delayed *Earl Godwin* sailed directly from refit at Holyhead to Guernsey where she arrived for trials on 26th January. Her maiden voyage was the 08.30 from Jersey and Guernsey to Weymouth on 26th January. Much of her cabin accommodation had been removed and replaced by rows of reclining seats.

The *Caesarea* left Weymouth for Dover on 3rd February. With the *Caledonian Princess* now a Channel Islands vessel, she was sent to Immingham to be converted into a one class ship and to have her inside seating spaces extended by 300. The ship was late back from refit but took up service again on 12th May. The *Sarnia's* season consisted of a round sailing to Guernsey on Wednesdays and crossings to both islands each weekend.

After completion of a charter to Lion Ferry, the twelve year old Townsend Thoresen ferry *Viking II* was duly purchased by Lloyd's Leasing Ltd. on behalf of the B.R.B. and arrived at Holyhead on 22nd December for conversion. As the *Earl William*, she was due to open the new Portsmouth–Channel Islands route on 31st October 1977.

Holyhead: The *Cambria* was sold to the Orri Navigation Company of Saudi Arabia for £350,000 and renamed *Altaif*. After being laid up at Barrow, she arrived in the Mersey on 17th January to take on bunkers at Tranmere. She foundered in Suez Roads in January 1981.

Arriving in thick fog early on 18th March, the *Avalon* extensively damaged her bow and went off service for two weeks. Her deep draught made berthing in the inner harbour difficult during periods of low water when she was frequently required to sail up to an hour early. The *Dover* was switched from Fishguard to deputise while the spare *Maid of Kent* moved to the St. George's Channel route.

The 16 year old livestock/cargo ship *Slieve Donard* was sold for £200,000 to Nashar Saudi Lines of Jeddah and was towed from Holyhead to Birkenhead on 1st July. A further £300,000 was spent on refitting the vessel which was renamed *Arabi* for service transporting up to 8,000 sheep between Somalia, India and Saudi Arabia. She was broken up at Gadani Beach, Pakistan, in April 1987.

After a delay of 24 hours, the new vehicle ferry *St. Columba* was launched at Aalborg on 17th July.

At 00.15 on 3rd October, the *Hibernia* completed her final sailing on the 20.45 from Dun Laoghaire. She was sold to Greek owners, Agapitos Bros., and was renamed *Express Apollon*. She sailed from Holyhead, to the Mersey, to take on bunkers on 1st December. The vessel was broken up at Mumbai, India in 1981.

Heysham: The chartered freight vessel *Penda*, en-route from Belfast to Heysham, had a serious engine room fire on 19th October. After discharging her cargo she sailed to Holyhead for repairs and the *Anderida* took up the link as from 26th October.

◆ **1977**

Harwich: The oldest of the four Harwich–Zeebrugge train ferries, *Suffolk Ferry* (built for the L.N.E.R. in 1947) was retained in service due to the boom in traffic on the route. The newest of the four ships, the *Cambridge Ferry* of 1963, received a £91,000 extension to her boat deck to allow 25 more trade cars to be carried. Modifications were also made to her stern to allow her to fit the Dunkerque linkspan.

Dover: Sealink's French subsidiary the Angleterre-Lorraine-Alsace Societe Anonyme de Navigation (A.L.A.) became wholly owned by the British Railways Board on 23rd March.

The Newhaven ferry *Senlac* arrived for overhaul in

The **Cambria** at Dun Laoghaire. (Ferry Publications Library)

Dover's Wellington Dock on 27th December while the *Earl Leofric* deputised at Newhaven.

Newhaven: The *Villandry* re-entered service during the spring after conversion to drive-through operations. The *Senlac* made a special sailing to be present at the Jubilee Naval Review at Spithead on 28th June.

On 6th September the *Valencay* when an hour out from Newhaven suffered damage to one of her twin screws resulting in contact with a rudder. The ship completed the voyage to Dieppe going astern at 6 knots before sailing to Le Havre for repairs and conversion to drive-through operations.

Channel Islands: On 28th June the *Sarnia* was present at the Jubilee Naval Review at Spithead. On 4th September the classic passenger ship made her final sailing between the Channel Islands and Weymouth and six days later operated a charter to Guernsey.

Following the withdrawal of the passenger vessels, all the Channel Island sailings were to be operated by car ferries, with the *Caledonian Princess* and *Earl Godwin* operating from Weymouth followed by the newly acquired *Earl William* establishing a new service from Portsmouth.

The new service from Portsmouth to the Channel Islands finally started on 8th November 1977 following two separate bouts of industrial action involving the crews of the *Earl Godwin* who were to operate the service initially prior to the arrival of the *Earl William*.

Fishguard: During May, the *Anderida* switched to the Rosslare route from Dover thereby allowing the charter of the *Preseli* to be terminated. She was required there to operate with the *Duke of Lancaster* which lacked freight capacity. It had initially been planned to send the converted *Dover* (*Earl Siward*) to the link. The Rosslare route lost £97,000 in 1976. The *Preseli* took up charter to P&O for which she was renamed *Pointer* on the Ardrossan-Belfast service.

Holyhead: The new *St. Columba* arrived at Holyhead on 6th April and took up service on 2nd May.

Stranraer: It was announced in the autumn that a new passenger/ car ferry would be ordered from Harland & Wolff for delivery in spring 1979, for the Stranraer-Larne service. The new vessel would be a twin-level drive on/ drive off ship, designed to carry 600 passengers and 300 cars or 60 commercial vehicles. To enable the new ship to be used on the service, a new twin-level berth had to be provided at Larne as part of a £1 million expansion programme.

◆ 1978

Harwich: S.M.Z's new *Prinses Beatrix* was launched on 14th January. After undertaking trials off the coast of Norway she entered service on 24th June. The new vessel replaced the passenger-only ship *Koningin Wilhelmina* which was withdrawn from service on 28th June after which she was sold to Greek owners. She remains in service today as the *Panagia Tinoy*.

Dover: The *Normannia* operated her final sailings from the port on 20th January before sailing to Weymouth where she finished her career. With the *Lord Warden* based at Fishguard for the summer, this was the first peacetime summer since 1888 that the Dover Strait had not boasted a ship built at the famous Denny of Dumbarton shipyard. The 'Warden' returned to Dover in November to operate a three week stint on the Boulogne route vice the *Compiegne*. Her final sailing was on 8th December.

Folkestone: The *Vortigern's* annual refit at Middlesbrough included the £200,000 conversion of her after boat deck garage (in use when the ship operated as a train ferry) to a passenger lounge. The ship's passenger certificate was raised from 1,000 to 1,350 and two extra lifeboats were fitted.

Newhaven: The German ro-ro vessel *Ro-Ro Cimbria* was chartered for a three week period early in the year to assist the *Caledonian Princess*.

Channel Islands: After numerous delays, the *Earl William* finally made her debut at Portsmouth on 16th January. This allowed the *Earl Godwin* to return to Weymouth which allowed the *Caledonian Princess* to proceed to Newhaven where she released the *Earl Leofric*.

Further problems faced the local management when the *Earl Godwin* was involved in an industrial dispute at Immingham Docks. Although work on the ship was nearly complete, it was not possible for her to be released from the docks as lock-gate operators went on strike. The continued industrial dispute at Immingham forced Sealink to bring the sale-listed *Normannia* into service on the Channel Islands service until 31st March. Taking her place came the chartered Townsend Thoresen ferry *Viking Victory*.

With the *Caledonian Princess* requiring dry-docking during April, the *Normannia* was again pressed into service with the help of the *Caesarea* which also made an unexpected return to the route to increase capacity. The *Normannia* ceased to carry passengers from 17th April but the *Caledonian Princess* returned on 1st May followed by the *Earl Godwin* four days later after which things returned to normal.

The *Maid of Kent's* late arrival from overhaul saw the *Lord Warden* called up from lay-by at Newhaven to run the Cherbourg link over Easter.

During June the *Sarnia* and *Normannia* were sold. The *Normannia* was purchased by Red Sea Ferries of Dubai for use on one of their existing routes in the Persian Gulf. Meanwhile, the *Sarnia* was purchased by Channel Cruise Lines Limited of St. Peter Port, Guernsey to operate as a duty-free cruise vessel trading out of Continental ports. Sales of both ships were to experience difficulties.

The sale of the *Normannia* to Arab interests as a pilgrim ship fell through at the eleventh hour prior to her being towed to Rotterdam for remedial work. The *Sarnia* left Weymouth on 24th May for Immingham after being sold to Channel Cruise Lines Ltd. Renamed *Aquamart*, the ship began service in mid-July in her new role of excursion ship/entertainment complex/duty-free ship operating out of Dunkerque and Ostend. After the initial voyages, serious problems developed over the duty-free entitlement of passengers and protests from Ostend traders resulted in a ruling that day-trippers were not eligible to land with duty-free purchases. The vessel's owners claimed that this was opposite to the original assurances and agreements reached before the sailings commenced. Following her short-lived and controversial career, the vessel arrived in the West India Docks at London for lay-up on 4th August.

Following the unsuccessful sale of the *Normannia* she was eventually sold again. The vessel sailed under her own steam and departed from Newhaven on 29th November for scrap in northern Spain.

On completion of her short stay on the Irish Sea, the *Maid of Kent* underwent a major refit at Holyhead, prior to returning to the Weymouth–Cherbourg service for the following year. During 1978, the company were to see a 30% increase in car and passenger traffic on their Dorset–Normandy service.

Fishguard: Following the printing of their first brochure, Sealink made the surprise announcement that the *Lord Warden* would be employed on a new eight week ferry link between Fishguard and Dun Laoghaire as from July. The vessel would also offer an additional night sailing to Rosslare.

Later in the summer, Sealink announced that they had ordered a new ferry for the Fishguard–Rosslare service. The vessel would be designed on similar lines to that of the earlier ordered Stranraer and Dover vessels.

Speculation that Sealink might be on the verge of chartering or purchasing an additional vessel for their Irish Sea operations was heightened in September when the Swedish-registered ferry *Stena Nordica* undertook trials at Fishguard and Rosslare on 4th-5th September.

The Fishguard–Waterford container service had been losing money for some time and in its final few years a number of well-known freight vessels appeared on the route. The former A.H.L. vessel *Harrogate* had been replaced by the

Container Enterprise in 1971 and in August 1973 the *Isle of Ely* had taken up the route. The year 1976 saw the *Container Venturer* on the service which Sealink claimed was losing some £300,000 a year. After ridding themselves of their statutory obligation to operate the Waterford service, the way was free for the route to close on 19th March.

The *Container Enterprise* was renamed *Isacar I* while the 'Venturer' became the *Trupial*. They are still in service as the *Sea Container* and *Sea Mist*.

Holyhead: Little more than a year after entering service for Sealink between Holyhead and Dun Laoghaire, the *St. Columba* carried her millionth passenger. The new vessel was also to attract more holidaymakers wanting to take their cars to Ireland. The boom in traffic across the Irish Sea showed healthy increases in passengers and vehicles on the Holyhead-

Dun Laoghaire route. Meanwhile, Sealink chartered the freighter *Transbaltica* to relieve the *St. Columba* of some of her lorry traffic. During the autumn, the *Dalriada* arrived in place of the *Transbaltica* to support the *St. Columba*.

The *Duke of Lancaster* took over the Holyhead–Dun Laoghaire service at the beginning of October when Sealink were forced to withdraw the *St. Columba* with propeller shaft problems. The `Duke' was employed to handle passengers and cars while the *Dalriada* supported her in a freight mode. During the Irish Public Holiday weekend at the end of October, the *Maid of Kent* was brought into service to provide additional capacity. The *St. Columba* eventually returned to service on 8th November. Meanwhile the *Lord Warden* returned to the Dover Strait.

The **Lord Warden** *leaving Dover in 1977. (Ferry Publications Library)*

Heysham: The freight service between Heysham and Belfast was reorganised in November when the 'Coastlink' lo–lo service ceased and a two ship ro–ro service using the displaced Stranraer vessels *Penda* and *Dalriada* commenced.

Stranraer: The new ro-ro ferry *Darnia* entered service on the Stranraer-Larne service on 10th August, replacing the *Dalriada*. She was built in Austria and completed in Romania as the *Stena Topper* before being chartered by British Transport Ship Management (Scotland) from James Fisher & Sons of Barrow. Following trials at both ports, she went immediately to Harland & Wolff to have her passenger accommodation extended, the installation of stabilisers and a high-capacity vehicle lift. The vessel was named after the ancient kingdom of Antrim. With a service speed of 17.5 knots, the *Darnia* made the crossing in two and a quarter hours and offered a third more capacity than the *Dalriada*. Following her arrival, Sealink were able to operate a daily schedule of up to 22 sailings a day with the *Antrim Princess*, *Ailsa Princess* and the *Ulidia*. For the first time on the route, all four ships were to carry the British flag and manned by British crews. Meanwhile, it was announced that the first of the vessels under construction at Harland & Wolff for the Stranraer service would be named *Galloway Princess*.

◆ 1979

The first day of 1979 saw the creation of Sealink U.K. Ltd, a wholly-owned subsidiary of the British Railways Board, who were to take the company to its privatisation and eventual purchase by Sea Containers (trading as Sealink British Ferries) in 1984.

In its first year, Sealink U.K. made a profit of £13.7 million only £500,000 better than 1978 and somewhat below anticipated budgets. Increased competition from other ferry operators especially on the cross-Channel services coupled with soaring oil fuel prices contributed to the lower than expected profits.

Dover: The summer saw the Dover–Calais service operated by the steamers *Earl Leofric* and *Earl Siward* in the company of the French ferry *Chartres* while the Dover–Boulogne service was being worked by the French vessels *Compiegne* and *Chantilly*. Early in the year an order

was made for two new larger ferries for 1980, while during the summer the French ordered a new vessel with similar capacity.

Lady Parker (wife of B.R. Chairman Sir Peter Parker) named the first new ship *St. Anselm* at Harland & Wolff, Belfast on 4th December although gale force winds prevented the ship from being launched until the following day.

Channel Islands: On the foggy afternoon of 20th January, the former Sealink ship *Sarnia*, later trading as the *Aquamart*, renamed *Golden Star* (and later *Saudi Golden Star*) was towed from London to Greece for further service. She was broken up at Gadani Beach, Pakistan in February 1987.

There was to be a significant increase in sea traffic to the Channel Islands during 1978, the figures for Jersey showing a 12% increase in traffic over the previous year. The introduction of the new Portsmouth route and an entirely car ferry orientated service had proved that Sealink had introduced the link for those who wanted their holidays on the Islands. In February, the Weymouth service was suspended after the Portsmouth-Channel Islands ferry *Earl William* was taken out of service for ten weeks following a chain becoming entangled on the propeller, requiring the fitting of a new shaft. The *Earl Godwin* was transferred from

*The former Sealink ship **Duke of Lancaster** at Llanerch-y-Mor in 1980. (John Collins)*

*The **Maid of Kent** leaving Dover for Boulogne. (John Hendy)*

*The **Earl William** arriving at Weymouth In 1983. (Miles Cowsill)*

Weymouth to deputise on the route. Sealink had hoped that they would be able to maintain a Weymouth service to the Islands by using the *Maid of Kent* but her overhaul at Holyhead was to take longer than anticipated. The Weymouth service therefore was suspended and the sailings of the *Earl Godwin* from Portsmouth were increased to six per week during the closure. The *Earl Godwin* maintained the Portsmouth operation until the end of February.

The *Maid of Kent* resumed the Cherbourg service from Weymouth on 6th April after receiving considerable internal improvements at Holyhead.

Fishguard: On 17th February, the *Anderida* went off service with an engine room fire whilst on passage from Rosslare. Subsequently the route was short of cargo capacity until the arrival on station of the chartered sister to the *Stena Nordica*, the *Stena Normandica* on 3rd March. She was chartered for a nineteen month period until the arrival of the new ship then under construction at Belfast. On her arrival the vessel entered service in place of the *Avalon* and *Anderida* both of which were released from the port.

By the early summer the company was claiming that the passenger and freight figures on the link had seen some 10% increase since the introduction of the new ship. Sadly, the

Stena Normandica was to encounter major mechanical problems in June which eventually meant that the *Avalon* had to return to Fishguard from Holyhead while she underwent major engine repairs. The company chartered the ro-ro vessel *Ilkka* (60 lorries) from Tejo Shipping of Jersey during this period. She was released when the 'Normandica' finally returned on 23rd September.

Holyhead: During March, the chartered *Stena Timer* (a sister of the *Darnia*) was brought into service at Holyhead to support the *Avalon* with freight sailings. She had previously operated as P&O's *Jaguar* on their Fleetwood–Larne service. A second visit was made by the ship from 21st May as a back-up to the *St. Columba* and she remained on the service until 25th September.

Meanwhile the *Lord Warden* returned to the Holyhead/ Fishguard–Dun Laoghaire service but not on the Rosslare route as in the previous season. She completed her service with a sailing from Dun Laoghaire to Holyhead on 8th September before sailing to Newhaven two days later.

The *St. Columba* failed with gear-box troubles on 30th October when passengers and cars were diverted to the Fishguard and Liverpool routes. The *Maid of Kent* was introduced the following day and was assisted by the *Stena Timer* before the 'Columba' resumed within the week.

The **Galloway Princess** enters the water for the first time at Belfast. *(Jim Ashby collection)*

Heysham: Sealink U.K. Ltd (60%) and Barrow shipowners James Fisher & Son Ltd. (40%) purchased the independent company Manx Line late in 1979. The company had commenced ro–ro operations on the Heysham–Douglas (Isle of Man) link on 26th August 1978 with their former Aznar Line vessel *Monte Castillo* which they had renamed *Manx Viking* (3,589 gross tons). The vessel was built in Spain during 1976 and boasted capacity for 192 cars and 777 passengers. All sorts of problems had beset the new company including an on-board fire during the ship's fitting out at Leith and diverse mechanical problems which meant an extremely unreliable service. On 1st December 1978, their Douglas linkspan had sunk in a gale which had plunged the new company into further financial problems. The full linkspan service did not recommence until 29th June 1980 after which the lo–lo container vessel *Eden Fisher* stood down.

As from summer 1980, the Heysham–Douglas route was marketed as Sealink Manx Line. More mechanical problems with the *Manx Viking* saw the *Dalriada* in operation from 9th November until 3rd December. The *Earl William* was ear-marked to operate a passenger service during this period but broke down herself and was unable to make the voyage northwards.

Stranraer: The new ferry, the *Galloway Princess*, for the Stranraer-Larne service was launched without ceremony or naming at Harland & Wolff on 24th May. The anticipated completion of the vessel at the time was October. The chartered *Stena Timer* arrived at Stranraer on 9th January to cover the period of the local overhauls and following her spell at Holyhead duly returned to Stranraer on 13th April.

Disposals: Meanwhile, the *Duke of Lancaster* was sold by Sealink for static use at Llanerch-y-Mor, near Mostyn, in North Wales. The vessel, which had last operated for the company on 9th November 1978, while standing in for the *St. Columba*, was purchased by Empirewise of Liverpool and was towed from lay-up at Barrow, arriving in her new home on 10th August 1979. There had been speculation that she might be used to supplement sailings of Manx Line between

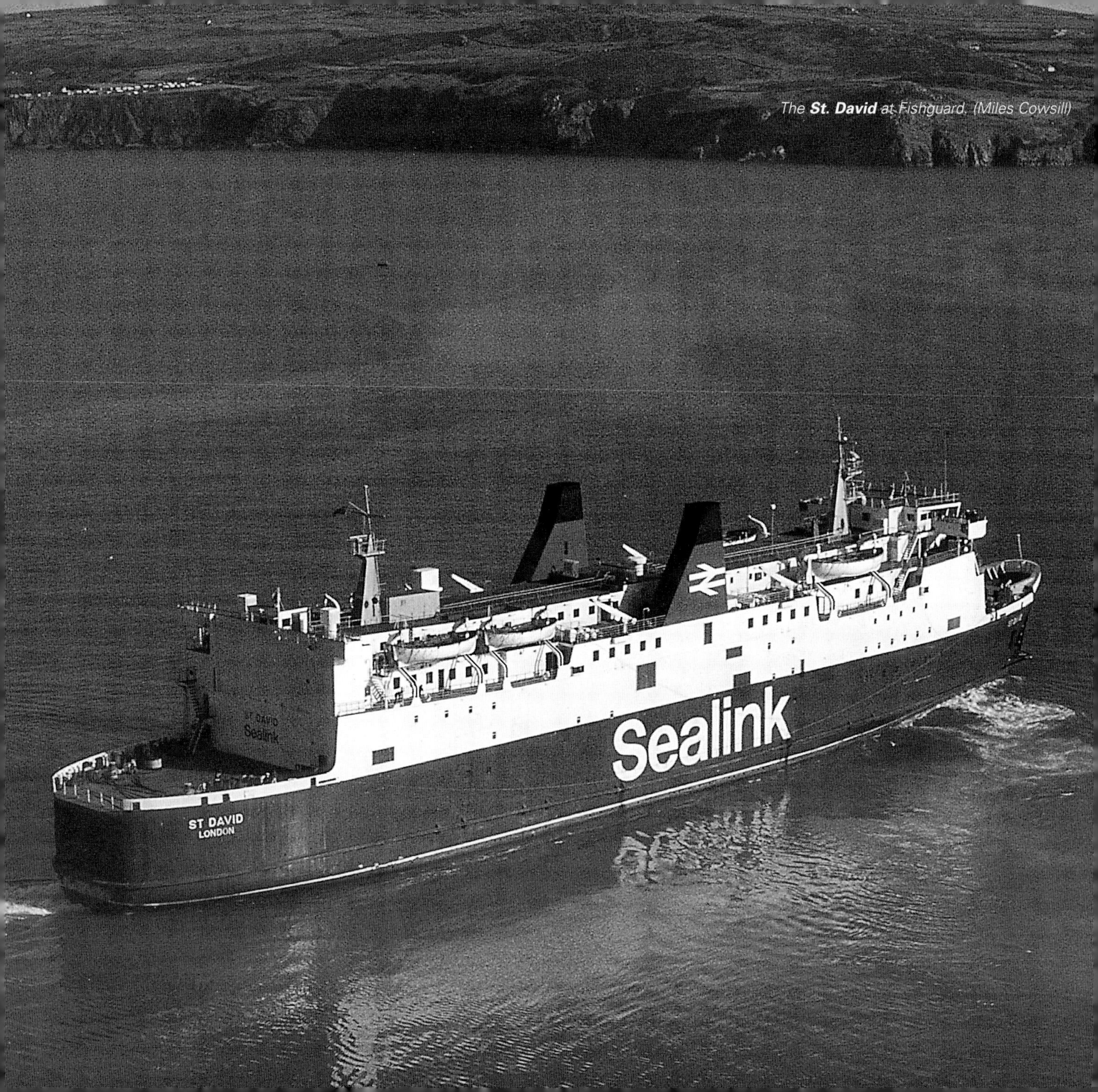

The **St. David** at Fishguard. (Miles Cowsill)

Heysham and Douglas prior to her disposal.

At the end of the summer season, Sealink announced that the turbine steamer *Lord Warden* would be placed on the sale list as no further work could be found for the vessel. It had originally been planned to operate her at Fishguard in place of the *Avalon*, following the mechanical problems of the *Stena Normandica*. The *Lord Warden* was eventually sold to the Baboud Trading and Shipping Agency of Jeddah, Saudi Arabia, and on 2nd January 1980, sailed from Southampton as the *Al Zaher* for short-lived service in the Red Sea. She arrived at Gadani Beach in Pakistan for breaking on 25th April 1981.

◆ 1980

On 14th July, the Transport Minister announced plans to denationalise the shipping, hovercraft and hotels sections of British Rail "within the next two or three years." The injection of private capital into the non-rail subsidiaries was to allow them far more latitude although British Rail would be allowed to keep a minority shareholding in the businesses.

Harwich: Plans were announced in the spring to build two new £15 million train ferries for the Harwich–Zeebrugge route, to be delivered in 1983 and 1985. To fill the gap, Sealink completed a two year charter of the *Stena Shipper* (3,220 gross tons) and installed railway lines on her vehicle deck. The larger 100 wagon ships would require a larger berth and plans were drawn up for this to be constructed at Parkeston Quay. The *Speedlink Vanguard* was built in 1973 as the Union Steamship Co's *Union Wellington* before being sold to Greece as the Argharis Line's *Alpha Express*. This company collapsed in 1979 when Stena purchased the ship.

The arrival of the new vessel for berthing trials from the Tees on 20th August saw the end of the *Suffolk Ferry* which had sailed over one million miles since August 1947. She left Harwich for Belgian breakers in tow of the tug *Engeland* on 25th November. The *Norfolk Ferry* (1951) was also withdrawn from regular service and placed in reserve.

During November Sealink ended their charter of the James Fisher cargo vessel *Brathay Fisher* (3,604 gross tons). The ship had been built in 1971 and had served both the Harwich–Dunkerque and, from March 1977, Harwich–Zeebrugge links during her career with the

company. On the latter route she had sailed with the former Holyhead vessel *Rhodri Mawr*.

Dover: At 12.30 on 18th March, Miss Tina Heath (a presenter on the B.B.C. children's programme 'Blue Peter') named the second Dover ship, *St. Christopher*. Once again the launch was delayed by gales and it was not until two days later that the ship slipped into Belfast Lough. It was now obvious that the two new ships would not be ready for the 1980 season while competitors Townsend Thoresen introduced three new Bremerhaven-built 'Spirit' class vessels. The *St. Anselm* (7,003 gross tons) was due in service at 11.30 on 1st July while the 'Christopher' should have followed on the 01.00 on 28th September. As it was, the first ship under the command of Captain John Arthur, previously promoted to Sealink Fleet Commodore, finally arrived in her home port on 24th October. The ship's maiden voyage was the 07.00 on 27th October thereby replacing the *Earl Leofric* which sailed to lay-up at Newhaven. However the *Earl Siward* stripped some turbine blades on 2nd November and the 'Leofric' was reactivated and remained in service until 17th December after which she again retired to Newhaven. Plans to bring the *Antrim Princess* to Dover, vice the *Earl Siward*, until the entry of the *St. Christopher* were shelved.

The first S.N.C.F. car ferry *Compiegne* also completed her advertised sailings during the year finishing with the 22.30 from Dover to Boulogne on 27th September. Meanwhile the new *Cote d'Azur* was launched in heavy rain at Le Havre on 22nd December.

The final running of the famous 'Night Ferry' through passenger train linking London (Victoria) with Brussels and Paris via the Dover–Dunkerque train ferry duly took place on 31st October. The service commenced in October 1936.

Folkestone: The *Caesarea's* final season commenced on 16th May when she left the Wellington Dock following her overhaul. For the remainder of the month she was used on a when and where required basis but took up scheduled sailings on 1st June. Until 1st July she was used between Calais–Folkestone–Boulogne and thereafter (until 27th September) added Boulogne–Dover–Calais to her roster. A series of 'Farewell' cruises were organised from Dover before a final charter by the ship's Master, Captain Mike Bodiam, on behalf of the local branch of the R.N.L.I.

The turbine crossed for the last time between Folkestone and Boulogne on 4th October bringing to an end 159 years of steam driven passenger vessels. A sale to Hong Kong owners Superluck Enterprises was quickly confirmed and as the *Aesarea* the ship sailed from Newhaven on 20th December.

Newhaven: A fire in the *Senlac's* alternator room while alongside at Dieppe on 13th June caused immediate evacuation of almost 1,000 passengers. Fortunately, the ship's internal sprinkler system extinguished the flames but she had to be withdrawn from service and sent to Avonmouth for repairs. The spare Stranraer–Larne freight *Ulidia* which was laid up at Newhaven at the time was hastily prepared to briefly take up the service as soon as possible. With the *Valencay* away being converted to drive-through operations, the link badly required an extra passenger-carrying ship and a charter was arranged with Townsend

Thoresen for their *Free Enterprise II*. Although ideal for passengers and cars, the chartered vessel's freight capacity was poor, so from July until 18th August the sale-listed Irish freighter *Dundalk* (later Sealink's *St. Cybi*) was chartered until the *Senlac* returned.

During early August, striking French fishermen closed every port on the country's northern coast from Brittany through to Dunkerque. The French ferry *Valencay* was unable to dock at her home port on 14th August when steel cables were put across the mouth of the harbour by the militant fishermen. The continued blockade of the ports brought frustration to thousands of holidaymakers and a short truce lasted some 21 hours at the port of Cherbourg, which allowed ferry companies to get passengers home. The Newhaven trio, the *Senlac*, *Villandry* and *Valencay* were employed during this period to operate to and from Cherbourg. The *Senlac* also operated on certain days to Ostend from Newhaven.

Awaiting disposal at Newhaven in November 1980 are the **Earl Leofric** *(right) and* **Casearea**. *(John Hendy)*

*The chartered **Stena Timer** leaving Holyhead. (D. Roberts)*

*The **Stena Normandica** at Rosslare. (Miles Cowsill)*

Channel Islands: The continued success of the new Portsmouth–Channel Islands service saw Sealink acquire a further vessel to operate instead of the *Earl William*. The Finnish Viking Line vessel *Viking 4* was acquired by W & G Industrial Leasing Ltd. in 1980 and was sent to Bremerhaven where she was re-engined and extensively altered for her new career.

Sealink were to experience troubles on their Weymouth-Channel Islands services for most of May, when the sailings had to be shared by the *Caledonian Princess* and the hurriedly chartered Townsend Thoresen vessel *Free Enterprise II*. The Townsend Thoresen ship had been summoned from Dover following the engine failure of the *Earl William*, which meant that the *Earl Godwin* had to be switched from Weymouth to Portsmouth. The 'FE II' maintained the link until 11th June.

Fishguard: The success of the *Stena Normandica* on the Fishguard–Rosslare service brought speculation that she would be retained on the route with an extended charter from Stena Line, while the new vessel being built for the route, confirmed as the *St. David*, might well be used at Holyhead to cope with the increased freight and passenger traffic at the Anglesey port.

Holyhead: The chartered ro–ro vessel *Stena Timer* left Holyhead for Stranraer on 7th February after assisting the *Avalon* to cover for the *St. Columba* which was late back from her Clydeside overhaul.

The Holyhead–Dun Laoghaire route was seriously disrupted after the *St. Columba* suffered a further serious engine failure at the Irish port on 21st May with all sailings cancelled until the *Avalon* could be brought into service the following day. The *Avalon* then experienced boiler troubles and had to be withdrawn from operations. Cargo was shifted by using the *Lagan Bridge* (from Heysham) and even the Harwich train ferry *Cambridge Ferry* which was in the port undergoing overhaul at this time. The *Ailsa Princess* was sent from Stranraer to take up the service as from 31st May–her first ever spell away from the route for which she was built. Three days later the *Avalon* was repaired and she was able to resume services in the absence of the *St. Columba* which was off service for three weeks. She eventually returned to service on the 12th June.

On 25th September, the £16 million *St. David*, the last of the quartet of ferries ordered at Harland & Wolff, was duly launched at Belfast. Already some four months behind schedule, it was still uncertain whether or not the vessel would be employed on the Fishguard–Rosslare service as originally planned. At the time that the *St. David* was named by Mrs. Ruth Fowler, wife of British Railways Board member Mr. Derek Fowler, the three other ships of the series were also at Belfast. The short sea sisters the *St. Anselm* and *St. Christopher* were fitting-out while the slightly smaller *Galloway Princess* was receiving shaft and propeller attention in dry dock.

After completing Holyhead-Dun Laoghaire relief sailings on 8th September, the *Avalon* was sent for lay-up at Barrow on 24th September with an uncertain future. The ship was later sold for scrap at Gadani Beach in Pakistan and left as the *Valon* in December.

Heysham: Sealink's Belfast–Heysham freight service continued to see further growth with the introduction of new tonnage. The *Lagan Bridge* (ex. *Ilkka*) and *Lune Bridge* (ex. *Anu*) replaced the previous vessels *Dalriada* and *Penda*. The two new ships, both completed in Norway in 1972, had seen previous service in British waters, the *Ilkka* with Sealink and the other for Townsend Thoresen as the *Anu*. Both new ships made regular weekend sailings from Holyhead during the summer period and both made calls at Douglas (Isle of Man) to assist with the Manx Line service.

The *Dalriada* was returned to Stena and was renamed *Stena Trader*. She was soon back in British waters on charter to Townsend Thoresen at Portsmouth and Southampton while, after her spell at Stranraer, the *Penda* left the Holyhead dry dock on 28th May as P&O Ferries *n.f. Jaguar* for service between Southampton and Le Havre. She was sent to Liverpool's Princes Dock to lay-up in October before commencing her association with the Isle of Man Steam Packet Company for whom she presently operates as the *Peveril*.

In a surprise move Sealink announced in September that the Heysham–Belfast freight ro-ro service would close on 13th December. The route had been under threat previously but this appeared to have been removed when two larger chartered ships, *Lagan Bridge* and *Lune Bridge*, were introduced the previous January. Sealink claimed that the service had operated at a considerable loss for some time and that the estimated deficit in 1980 would exceed £1 million. Efforts were made to encourage customers to switch their business to the Stranraer–Larne vehicle ferry or Holyhead–Belfast container service.

The *Lune Bridge* completed the final outward sailing while

The **Lune Bridge** *arriving at Heysham. (D.I. Harmsworth)*

the *Lagan Bridge* completed the last eastbound crossing before both ships sailed to Clydedock Engineering on 16th December. They were renamed *Lady Catherine* and *Lady Tone*.

In October, Sealink increased its holding in the former Manx Line to 85%.

Stranraer: With the freighter *Ulidia* off service with gearbox troubles early in the year, the spare *Penda* (from Heysham) took her place while the *Stena Timer* covered for her sister, the *Darnia*, during her period of overhaul. On the arrival of the new ship in May, the *Ulidia* was sent to lay-up at Newhaven.

Continued delays with the completion of the new Stranraer–Larne ship *Galloway Princess* saw the *Antrim Princess* and *Ailsa Princess* maintaining the link together.

Meanwhile, following the entry into service of the *Galloway Princess* (6,268 gross tons) at 08.30 on 1st May she too was to experience mechanical problems and was taken out of service for a week at the end of June.

 1981

Harwich: During the train ferry *Speedlink Vanguard's* first overhaul, and the subsequent overhauls of the *Essex Ferry* and *Cambridge Ferry*, the spare *Norfolk Ferry* was brought out of mothballs to deputise for a period of about two months and made her final voyage in October.

Dover: With the S.N.C.F. multi-purpose ferry *Chartres* delayed in dry dock, the freighter *Anderida* was reactivated from the Wellington Dock at Dover. She had been there since Christmas and it was planned to move her to Newhaven on 7th February. Fearing that the ship would be sold and that they would lose their jobs, the officers refused to move her and so S.N.C.F. responded by bringing back their sale listed *Compiegne*.

On 9th April the *Ulidia* arrived at Dover to lay-up with her half-sister *Anderida*. There were plans to charter them to Dutch owners for the Great Yarmouth–Harlingen service but this failed to materialise. The *Ulidia* was again removed to Newhaven on 8th July (returning to Dover on 12th September) while the *Anderida* briefly saw service again on 11th July thereby allowing the A.L.A. train ferry *Saint Eloi* to operate an afternoon passenger sailing to Boulogne. Both

ships were finally sold to Greek owners and left Dover as the *Auto Trader* (*Ulidia*) and *Truck Trader* (*Anderida*) on 2nd November.

The *St. Christopher* (Captain Edwin Venables) eventually left Dover on her maiden voyage to Calais with the 08.15 on 15th April. The new-look Calais link was duly revamped, 'The Flagship Service. '

On 31st May the much-travelled *Caledonian Princess* commenced her final season with Sealink and her one and only spell on the Dover Strait. Denny's last railway steamer was called back to the Channel Islands routes during June to deputise for the fire-stricken *Earl Granville* and Sealink briefly chartered the spare Townsend Thoresen ferry *Free Enterprise III* to deputise on the Dover Calais/ Boulogne links from 25th June.

In the worst gales of the season, the *Caledonian Princess* completed her Sealink service under the command of Captain Mike Bodiam with a round Dover (Western Docks)–Boulogne sailing on 26th September.

S.N.C.F.'s new *Cote d'Azur* entered service with the 07.15

The **Chantilly** seen on passage to Dover. (Miles Cowsill)

*Denny's last ferry for the nationalised railway company was Stranraer's **Caledonian Princess**. She ended her service at Dover in 1981 and is seen leaving for Boulogne during her last month in operation. (Andrew Jones)*

Top left: *The 'Golden Arrow' steamer* **Invicta** *arriving at Dover Admiralty Pier on her last day in service - 8th August 1972. (Andrew Jones)*

Top right: *The* **Invicta's** *replacement was the* **Horsa** *which is seen arriving at Boulogne on an afternoon sailing from Folkestone. (John May)*

Left: *Farewell Heysham. The* **Duke of Argyll** *makes her final departure from the port on 16th May 1975. (D.I. Harmsworth)*

Below: *The* **St. Christopher** *about to enter Dover Harbour. In order to distinguish her from sistership* **St. Anselm**, *but without her Master's knowledge, the forward bulwark was painted blue. (John May)*

Top left: The former Channel Islands steamer **Caesarea** spent the final five years of her career in the Dover Strait. Here she is alongside at a misty Boulogne Maritime. (Miles Cowsill)

Top right: The **Earl Godwin** was formerly the Swedish ferry **Svea Drott** and replaced the **Falaise** on the Channel Islands service. She is seen leaving Weymouth. (Miles Cowsill)

Below: Holyhead's **Stena Hibernia** was Sealink's oldest vehicle ferry in service during 1995. She was built as the **St. Columba** in 1977 and is seen leaving Fishguard during her only spell on the Irish Sea's southern corridor. (Miles Cowsill)

During summer 1981, the **Antrim Princess** was laid up at Newhaven with the **Ulidia**. *(John Hendy)*

Columba breaking down again, the new Dover vessel sailed directly from her builders to Rosslare for berthing trials and then to Holyhead to cover the absence of the *St. Columba* making her maiden commercial voyage on 17th March. On the return of the Danish-built ship, the *St. Christopher* relieved the *Stena Normandica* at Fishguard on 19th March. The *St. Christopher* was to prove an excellent vessel whilst at the Pembrokeshire port, especially during some very inclement weather at the start of April. On the return of the *Stena Normandica*, she then sailed south to join her sister the *St. Anselm* on the Dover-Calais `Flagship Service'.

Meanwhile, the *Earl Siward*, which had been sharing the Newhaven lay-up berth with her sister the *Earl Leofric*, was sent to Holyhead for dry docking before supporting the *St. Columba* with relief sailings as from 22nd June. This was necessary following further delays in the construction of the *St. David*, which was now earmarked as a Holyhead vessel.

The *Earl Siward* was eventually replaced on 9th July by the chartered Swedish ferry *Prinsessan Desiree* which remained on station until the entry into service of the new ship from Belfast at 09.00 on 10th August.

Sealink's *St. David* (Captain Idwal Pritchard), the last of the £64 million quartet of vessels built at Harland & Wolff, displaced the *St. Columba* from the Holyhead–Dun Laoghaire winter service. Within a very short period of time, it became clear that the new vessel would be a more economic unit for the winter schedules and the *St. Columba* was laid up.

The *St. David* differed from her near sisters at Dover as her restaurant was forward in an area occupied by the main bar in the Dover Strait vessels. At the time of the ship entering service, she also boasted a 55 seat cinema and a duty-free supermarket, which neither Dover vessel claimed. Like her half-sisters, the vessel also included specially designed internal ramps to give easier access to the upper vehicle deck as neither Holyhead nor Dun Laoghaire had double-deck linkspans. She was also fitted with a stern bridge for docking at the Anglesey port.

Heysham: The Sealink Manx Line service saw the Townsend Thoresen ferry *Viking III* on charter between 28th September and 15th October after the *Manx Viking* had again failed with gearbox troubles. The *Antrim Princess* took over the route from 16th October and it was not until 11th January 1982 that the errant vessel returned.

During the *Manx Viking's* overhaul, between 25th March and 8th April the Channel Islands vessel *Earl Godwin* deputised. She was followed by the charter of the Townsend Thoresen ferry *Viking Victory* until the Manx vessel returned in her new Sealink livery on 17th April.

◆ 1982

Harwich: At the time of the industrial troubles at Newhaven in January, it was announced that Sealink were to sell the *Norfolk Ferry* and *Essex Ferry*, put the *Cambridge Ferry* in reserve and operate a single daily service with the *Speedlink Vanguard* while closing the Dunkerque West route (with the 'Cambridge') as from 18th April. These events caused the cessation of all Sealink U.K. cross Channel links.

A six month charter of the Stena Line freighter *Stena Sailer* commenced in January. The former Irish ro-ro vessel was built in 1975 as the *Dundalk* and was used on the Hook service for the duration of her charter.

During the spring, the Harwich–Hook service was severely stretched after the Ministry of Defence requisitioned the seven year old *St. Edmund* to serve in the Falklands War. Fortunately, the spare D.F.D.S. ferry *Prinz Oberon* was on hand following the closure of the Harwich–Bremerhaven link and after a brief charter to S.M.Z., commenced her Sealink U.K. workings on 12th March.

The *St. Edmund* was refitted in Portsmouth and sailed for the South Atlantic on 18th May. The day before she arrived in the War Zone, the occupying Argentine forces had surrendered and as from 14th July, the Sealink vessel was employed in transporting some 1,500 defeated troops back to Puerto Madryn in Argentina thereby bringing about a whole new meaning to the slogan then in use back home, "Sealink will set you free." At the conclusion of this work, the vessel maintained a dual role as a ferry between the Falkland Islands and Ascension Island and as an accommodation ship in Port Stanley where she earned herself the nickname of the 'Stanley Hilton.'

On her return to England, the vessel was sold to the Ministry of Defence and renamed *Keren* for further work in the South Atlantic after which she was sold to Cenargo Navigation Ltd. and renamed *Scirocco*. A charter to British Channel Island Ferries commenced in February 1989 during

*'The Big One' - Sealink's publicity shot of the **Prinsessan Birgitta**. (Ferry Publications Library)*

which time the ship provided the link between Poole and Guernsey/ Jersey under the name of *Rozel*. At the termination of this work in January 1992, she returned to her owners for more charter work in the western Mediterranean.

Following the 'Edmund's' departure for the South Atlantic, Sealink announced that they were to charter the Stena Line vessel *Prinsessan Birgitta* (which they heralded as 'The Big One') in order to replace both her and her running partner, the *St. George*.

The vessel was originally built for Stena's rivals Sessan Line but after the line's purchase in January 1980, both the *Prinsessan Birgitta* (then simply known as Yard Number 909) and her year old sister, *Kronprinsessan Victoria* were spare.

With Sealink U.K. now operating with a single vessel, the Dutch partners S.M.Z. began to reappraise their operation.

The train ferry *Speedlink Vanguard* was in collision with the Townsend Thoresen ferry *European Gateway* some 2.5 miles off Harwich on the evening of 19th December. The Sealink ferry cut a 200 ft. gash in the side of the 'Gateway' as a result of which she rolled over onto her starboard side and sank. Six lives were lost. The *Speedlink Vanguard* returned to

The **Earl Siward** (ex. **Dover**) at berth 1, Dover Eastern Docks during November 1980. (John May)

During preparation for privatisation, the Directors of Sealink U.K. Ltd. commissioned a number of varying designs for a new company image and three of the unsuccessful versions are illustrated on the left of this page. (Jim Ashby collection)
Top Left: *A strange sight at Folkestone in April 1984 as the* **Hengist's** *funnel is in the course of being prepared for repainting in the new livery. (John May)*
Top right: *The successful design as displayed by the* **Horsa**. *(John May)*
Bottom Left: *The* **Hengist** *arriving at Boulogne in November 1989 in her British Ferries livery. (Miles Cowsill)*

embarked at Cammell Laird's Birkenhead yard, rails were installed on the main vehicle deck and the trials were carried out off the west coast of Scotland.

Heysham: The Sealink Manx Line vessel *Manx Viking* retired for annual overhaul between 12th February and 11th March during which time the *Ailsa Princess* was sent to deputise.

Stranraer: Following the departure of the *Ailsa Princess* from the Stranraer service, the *Darnia* received an extension to her accommodation to allow her to operate as a third passenger ship on the link with the *Galloway Princess* and *Antrim Princess*.

To cover for the absence of the *Darnia*, Sealink chartered the Brittany Ferries' freight vessel *Breizh Izel*. The French-registered ship arrived at Stranraer at the end of February.

Sealink also chartered the S.N.C.F. ferry *Villandry* to operate on their Stranraer–Larne service as from 7th June until early August. A Scottish crew was sent to collect the vessel from Dieppe and upon their arrival there, were told that under no circumstances would they be allowed to move the ship. The French union insisted that only a French crew could sail a French ship out of the country and the Sealink crew and officers had to make a return crossing to Newhaven as passengers before taking over the *Villandry* at Newhaven.

The industrial action at Newhaven also caused ships to be delayed for their winter overhauls. The *Galloway Princess* was snowbound at Avonmouth, which in turn delayed refits to the Stranraer vessels and the release of the *Ailsa Princess* for her new role at Weymouth.

◆ 1983

Harwich: Following a period of inactivity swinging at the buoys in the River Blackwater, Essex, both the *Norfolk Ferry* and *Essex Ferry* were sold during the spring. The 'Norfolk' was removed from her moorings by the tug *Banckerk* on 15th April and towed to Vlissingen for breaking. The *Essex Ferry* left the anchorage on 27th April and arrived two days later at Rainham, Kent, for breaking to main deck level at Medway Secondary Metals Ltd. Thereafter, on 10th June, the hulk, *Essex Ferry Pontoon* was towed by the tug *Sun London* to Haugesund, Norway, for use in raising the capsized oil rig

Alexander Kielland.

The chartered Stena Line vessel *Prinsessan Birgitta*, renamed *St. Nicholas*, made her maiden voyage on the Hook route on 10th June 1983 under the command of Captain Fred Wilkins. Union opposition to the removal of one ship brought about the Management threat to close down the Hook route and hand it over to S.M.Z. Fortunately sense prevailed.

The *St. George* had made her final sailing on 5th June before leaving Parkeston Quay for Immingham on 20th September. After the sale of the vessel to the Finnish company Folkline had fallen through, the *St. George* was sent to the Fal to lay-up. She was eventually sold to Ventouris Line of Greece late in 1984 and became their *Patra Express*. After a further sale to Sea Escapes in March 1990 she was renamed *Scandinavian Sky II* before crossing the Atlantic as the *Scandinavian Dawn* for day-trips from Port Everglades in Florida.

Dover: With the *St. Anselm* back at Harland & Wolff after Christmas 1982, receiving the extension to her accommodation, and expected back during March, Sealink switched the half-sister *St. David* to cover the period of the

*The **Essex Ferry** leaving Harwich for Zeebrugge. (Ferry Publications Library)*

'Christopher's' refit. She duly took up service under the command of Captain George Sutcliffe with the 13.00 to Calais on 31st March 1983.

With the *St. Anselm's* £750,000 refit complete she was called to work from Fishguard before arriving back in her home port on 31st March. The *St. Christopher* arrived back from Belfast on 9th June thereby releasing the 'David'.

Folkestone: With the *Horsa* late back from overhaul in March, the Belgian car ferry *Princesse Astrid* was chartered to await her return and operated both to Calais and Boulogne. Then, following a fire in her engine room workshop at Folkestone on 3rd April, the *Hengist* was withdrawn from service and the *Princesse Astrid* returned to operate her schedules three days later. On the occasions when more than 850 passengers were on offer (her maximum), the *Vortigern* was taken from the Dover–Dunkerque West train ferry service and switched to deputise. The British ship also operated the overnight freight runs to Ostend.

Newhaven: The *Senlac* refitted at Holyhead during late February when extensive work was carried out to her passenger accommodation, which included the conversion of her waiter-service restaurant into a lounge for lorry drivers and the conversion of her self-service restaurant to a cold buffet restaurant. The ship also had a new duty-free supermarket installed.

Meanwhile, between 9th–13th January, the Newhaven linkspan was out of action for repairs and the service was transferred to Folkestone instead, the crossing being scheduled to take just 15 minutes longer than that to Newhaven.

Fishguard/Holyhead: The *St. David* was sent to Stranraer to deputise for the refits of the vessels at the port. She then went to Fishguard to cover for the refit of the *Stena Normandica* before sailing to Dover to cover the conversion period of her near sister, *St Christopher*. This allowed the *St. Columba* to take up her key role again as the flagship at Holyhead.

Following the *Stena Normandica* returning to service, she promptly broke down but as luck would have it the *St. Anselm* was returning to Dover from Belfast following her major overhaul and she hastily took up the run for two days on 28th March.

The spare French ferry *Villandry* deputised for the *St. Columba* between 12th–13th August after the larger ship had gone off service with problems to her starboard engine.

Heysham: The *Manx Viking* suffered damage to her starboard engine during June and so the spare S.N.C.F. ferry *Villandry* was dispatched from Calais to deputise. She took up service on 24th June before finishing on 8th July.

Stranraer: On 9th December the *Antrim Princess* suffered a serious engine-room fire shortly after leaving Larne. R.A.F. helicopters lifted off some 128 passengers and 23 crew in a spectacular rescue operation as the vessel drifted to within a quarter of a mile of the Antrim coast. Townsend Thoresen's *Europic Ferry* was amongst the vessels which stood by and attempted unsuccessfully to take the *Antrim Princess* in tow. The Master and thirty crew remained on board and later the vessel was able to regain some power. After lying off Larne overnight, the *Antrim Princess* was towed to Belfast for repairs. The *St. David* was immediately sent to Stranraer to cover her absence, leaving the *St. Columba* to maintain the Holyhead–Dun Laoghaire service by herself. The 'Antrim' duly returned to service on 28th December.

◆ **1984**

In readiness for privatisation, on their reappearance from overhaul, units of the Sealink U.K. Ltd. fleet all appeared without the B.R. double arrow logo on their funnels. Four ships initially appeared with the all-white livery and blue funnels: the *St. Nicholas, Hengist, Horsa* and *Stena Normandica*. Of these vessels, the first and last of the four already had white hulls.

The new image was the work of H&P Associates who said of their work, "The symbol conveys authority and professionalism through its association with the badge of a naval officer. Use of an italicised letter form for the Sealink name combined with a strong horizontal stripe gives the impression of power and of purposeful direction. The corners of the lettering are radiused to soften the aggressiveness of the styling." And of the white hull they said, "White makes a vessel look larger, white offers greater visibility, white is associated with cleanliness, care and reliability, white doesn't show accumulated salt, white is suggestive of yachts and leisure, white projects a holiday atmosphere."

Front runners for purchase of Sealink U.K. Ltd. were a consortium headed by the National Freight Corporation, James Fisher & Sons Ltd. and senior Sealink management but July 1984 saw Sealink U.K. Ltd. sold to Sea Containers of Bermuda for just £66 million. The sale included 37 ships, 10 harbours and 24 routes. In future the company would trade as Sealink British Ferries and a subsidiary company British Ferries Ltd. was set-up. A general reappraisal was duly made of all routes and the ships which operated them.

In a letter to all Sealink staff, James Sherwood outlined his plans for the company. At Harwich the 'all clear' for the Bathside Bay development would see the area become Sea Containers' main U.K. base which would rival nearby Felixstowe. There was a possibility of switching one of the Harwich–Zeebrugge lo–lo vessels to Rotterdam while a new service to Duisburg (on the Rhine) was later announced. A further new passenger service to Denmark (and possibly other Baltic countries) was also planned. The Zeebrugge train ferry route was to expect a larger 75 wagon ship to replace

either the *Cambridge Ferry* or the *Speedlink Vanguard* which were both operated on behalf of the B.R.B.

Dover's Western Docks was to receive a large new terminal to which all train connected services would be operated and a Dover (Western Docks)–Boulogne route looked like being reinstated using the *St. David*. Folkestone would become a ro–ro port while Newhaven–Dieppe would be developed for the import of motor cars. The Isle of Wight links would have extra car ferries for Portsmouth and Lymington and the passenger-only Portsmouth–Ryde route would also receive new tonnage in the form of 400 seater Hovermarine craft. Of the Channel Islands routes, it was stated that they had always been a problem and had never made any money. The ships then in service would be replaced by two passenger/ car ferries with a single ro–ro ferry maintaining the link from Portsmouth.

On the Irish Sea, the Fishguard–Rosslare route would be expanded and larger Holyhead ferries were needed. The unprofitable lo–lo services from Holyhead to Belfast and Dublin would be revived by larger Sea Containers ships and Stranraer would see the replacement of the *Antrim Princess*.

*Celebrating the 'new image' - the **St. Nicholas** at Dover in March 1984. (John Hendy)*

After years of under-investment, it appeared that Sealink was about to be revitalised.

Harwich: Dutch partners S.M.Z. replaced their *Koningin Juliana* with the chartered Norwegian ferry *Peter Wessel* (renamed *Zeeland*) which entered service on 2nd April. The 'Juliana' was eventually sold to the Italian state company Navarma and was renamed *Moby Prince* for service to Sardinia. On 10th April 1991, the vessel was in collision with an anchored oil tanker, the resulting fireball engulfing the ship and all but one of the 140 people on board.

The Harwich train ferries retained their flame red funnels and B.R. arrow logos thus reflecting their continued charters to the B.R.B.

Dover: On 27th March, the Harwich–Hook vessel *St. Nicholas* arrived at Dover directly from overhaul in Dunkerque and painted in the new Sealink livery. Thereafter the ship sailed to Harwich with invited guests.

On 3rd June the new four ship Dover–Calais service commenced following the closure of the Folkestone–Calais service. Due to the delay of the *Champs Elysees*, the smaller *Chantilly* deputised and, in order to accommodate the rail-

The **Ailsa Princess** off Folkestone during October 1982. *(John Hendy)*

connected traffic, certain sailings were operated from the Western Docks linkspan. The 'Saints' proved inept on this service being unable to carry large numbers of foot passengers and their luggage and unable to berth stern-first, they berthed bow-in and reversed all lorry traffic on board. The Western Docks linkspan was rebuilt and enlarged during the 1984/ 85 winter.

The S.N.C.F. ferry *Champs Elysees* (9,069 gross tons) entered service to Calais with the 07.30 on 4th October after which the *Chantilly* was retired. Sea Containers' initial plans for the Dover Strait showed two new ferries for Dover–Calais with the twin 'Saint' class ferries being transferred to the Folkestone–Boulogne route.

Folkestone: The *Ailsa Princess* appeared a second time on the Folkestone routes as from 2nd January when she relieved the *Hengist* which sailed to Holyhead for shot-blasting in readiness for painting in the new Sealink livery. The ship arrived back on 22nd February sporting an all white hull and the 'Ailsa' departed the following day.

Newhaven: The need for a large freight vessel on the Newhaven–Dieppe service was fulfilled with the two year

S.M.Z's **Koningin Juliana** *passing Harwich for the Hook in 1978.* *(John Hendy)*

charter of the Brittany Ferries' vessel *Cornouailles* as from 13th January. The Norwegian-built vessel had a capacity for 500 passengers and 205 cars or 40 trailers and 30 cars. Her arrival saw the *Valencay* placed on the sale list although she had been scheduled to operate for the summer season. A further dispute on the route amongst French seamen delayed the new ship entering service until mid-February and the *Senlac* was left to maintain the link alone. The British ship was in trouble twice during the spring, firstly while berthing at Dieppe in thick fog on 1st March when she gashed herself against the quay and again on 27th April when two of her lifeboat davits collapsed without warning, leaving the lifeboat hanging over her side and a badly injured passenger.

Between times, French strikes at Dieppe saw the *Senlac* spend four days operating from Newhaven to Boulogne at the start of April. Meanwhile a 48 hour strike by members of the N.U.S. in protest against the pending privatisation of Sealink at the end of May saw the *Senlac* blocking the Newhaven linkspan and the S.N.C.F. ships having to operate to Folkestone.

S.N.C.F. were also anxious to spread their wings following a rival ferry service starting between Newhaven and Dieppe during April. They planned to start operating a new ferry service from Dieppe to Portsmouth in October 1984 using the displaced Dunkerque freight vessel *Transcontainer I*. Problems with the ship then saw S.N.C.F. look to their chartered *Cornouailles* to start the new operation but following a collision with the eastern pier at Newhaven in thick fog in October the vessel was forced to go off service with bow visor damage. The *Valencay* was again reactivated on the route. Further industrial action by French seamen saw the new service to Portsmouth being further postponed.

On 15th October came the news that Sea Containers, the new private owners of Sealink, intended to withdraw from the Newhaven–Dieppe route as from March 1985. The *Senlac* would be sold to S.N.C.F. who, under the terms of the joint agreement, already owned two-thirds of the ship. Her 260 officers and crew would be offered jobs at either Dover or Portsmouth. In a circular to all Sealink employees, James Sherwood, the Chairman of Sea Containers, wrote in the following January that as the *Senlac* was only able to make two round sailings each day (as opposed to four of the Dover/Folkestone vessels), this effectively meant that fares and retail and catering sales were half price. He also added in his

statement that the French received subsidies from the state, at regional and local levels, whereas Sealink received no subsidies at all.

Channel Islands: During 1984 the Jersey Authorities indicated that they would allow a rival ferry service from the Island to mainland Britain. A consortium of the Jersey based Huelin Renouf, Brittany Ferries, and the haulage company M.M.D. (Mainland Marketing Delivery) were considering plans to start a service between the Channel Islands and Britain using the now redundant *Penn-ar-Bed* from the fleet of Brittany Ferries. The French registered ship was unsuitable for this service as the British Department of Trade wanted a reduction in her freight capacity under the British flag. It was decided to look elsewhere for a suitable ship and the new service did not start until the following year. The new operation was eventually to see the demise of Sealink with their ferry operations to the Islands.

Sealink's new owners wasted little time in assessing the growth potential of their twenty four routes. One of the first suggestions by the Company was the withdrawal of the passenger service from Portsmouth to the Channel Islands and to concentrate the link to the Islands from Weymouth. James Sherwood, the President of Sea Containers, and now Chairman of Sealink, visiting Jersey and Guernsey in August, indicated to staff also that the *Ailsa Princess* should be joined by another ship to run an overnight service between Weymouth and Cherbourg. Nothing was to come of either of these plans. It was also indicated at one stage that the *Earl Granville* might be transferred to operate 'Orient Express' cruises from Venice.

The uncertainty of the Channel Islands operations from Weymouth and Portsmouth came hard on the heels of the announcement that the rival ferry service from mainland Britain to the Channel Islands would start as from April the following year. The new company claimed that they would run a daily service to the Islands throughout the year and that their fares would be far more competitive than those of Sealink.

Meanwhile, on 15th October, the *Earl Godwin* ran aground on the rocks east of the Elizabeth Castle breakwater at Jersey. The ship was eventually refloated and had to be withdrawn from service for repairs at Holyhead. The *Ailsa Princess* made her first visit to St. Helier for berthing trials on

*The **Earl Godwin** leaving St. Helier for Weymouth. (Miles Cowsill)*

8th October following the announcement of Sealink's new owners that both she and the *Earl Godwin* would operate a new pattern of daylight sailings between Weymouth and the Channel Islands as from April 1984. It was also disclosed that the *Earl William* and *Earl Granville* would undergo a major refurbishment in Denmark to start a new luxury ferry service from Portsmouth to the Channel Islands marketed under the banner of `Bateau De Luxe'. The new up-market service would go into direct competition to the new ferry service to be operated by the Jersey-based consortium of Channel Island Ferries. Both ships were sent to Denmark for £3.5 million refits, the *Earl William* sailed to Denmark in the early New Year and the *Earl Granville* on 26th January.

Meanwhile, the *Ailsa Princess* was converted for her new role to the Channel Islands and later renamed *Earl Harold*. The new `Sunliner' service to be operated by both the *Earl Harold* and *Earl Godwin* would operate from Weymouth at 13.15 and 15.15 with return sailings from the Islands at 07.15 from Guernsey and 07.30 from Jersey.

Holyhead: As the great privatisation debate continued, anxiety was being expressed by staff at Holyhead that the loss-making Holyhead–Dublin and Belfast container services would be closed as they were claimed to be losing something in the region of £2.8 million per year. The vessels the *Brian Boroime* and *Rhodri Mawr* were now too small for the Freightliner service and needed replacement; there was also a requirement for investment to revitalise the routes.

◆ 1985

On 25th October, the Belgian Government announced that as from 1st January 1986, R.M.T. would cease to be operational partners of Sealink U.K. Ltd. and would in future trade with rivals Townsend Thoresen. This came as a result of the failure to renegotiate Sealink's 15% of the Ostend route which new owners Sea Containers wished to increase to 50%. It was also made known that as from the end of 1985, the *St. David* would no longer be welcome in Ostend and so Sealink representatives immediately set to work attempting to secure berthing facilities at Zeebrugge. These were also denied.

With the building of the Channel Tunnel once more in the ascendancy, Sea Containers presented their own plans for its construction. The Government was informed that unless their

*The **Champs Elysees** seen under going berthing trials at Calais for the first time. The **Cote d' Azur** seen together at Calais. (Miles Cowsill)*

'Channel Expressway' was adopted then all 2,500 local employees would be made redundant.

The sense of uncertainty returned.

Harwich: On 1st October, Dutch partners S.M.Z. sold the *Prinses Beatrix* to French operators Brittany Ferries and immediately chartered her back to maintain the Hook service until the entry into service of the large new £40 million replacement vessel then under construction.

A question mark was raised concerning the future of the Harwich–Zeebrugge train ferry during the late summer when it was announced that British Ferries was seeking to replace both the *Cambridge Ferry* and the *Speedlink Vanguard*. French partners S.N.C.F. ordered a new super train ferry for the Dover–Dunkerque West link on 17th July. Sealink were contemplating building a sister ship and were known to be looking to divert traffic to Dover.

Dover: The *Champs Elysees* took up twice weekly sailings from Dover-Boulogne as from 19th January. On 1st July these became Saturday only sailings and were operated by the *St. David* as from 28th September. This vessel had been transferred to the Dover station as from 20th March to operate the Ostend service after the closure of the Folkestone–Ostend route. At this time Sealink U.K. Ltd. held a 15% share in the route and stated that they wished to expand their share to 50%. Objecting to the manner in which Sealink's new owners conducted their business, the Belgians duly entered into a trading agreement with Townsend Thoresen which took effect from 1st January 1986 after which Sealink were barred from Ostend.

The *Vortigern* commenced a new twice daily ro–ro service in March between Dover Western Docks and Dunkerque West.

The Dover–Dunkerque train ferry service became freight only after the S.N.C.F. vessel *Saint-Germain* and Sealink U.K's French-flag ferry *Saint Eloi* terminated passenger and car operations on 20th February and 27th September respectively.

On 17th July S.N.C.F. ordered their new super-train ferry from the Normed yard at Dunkerque. New linkspans were to be built to accommodate her in Dover and Dunkerque West. Plans were put in hand to stretch the *Saint Eloi* by lengthening her by 30 metres and also to insert a 5.2 metre extra deck for service in the English Channel with the new train ferry. Further plans to lift but not stretch the ship were made and, thus modified, there were moves to transfer her to the Fishguard–Rosslare route.

At an auction near Piraeus on 30th June, representatives of Sealink U.K. Ltd. successfully bid about $4.5 million for the Greek ro–ro vessel *Easy Rider* (5,072 gross tons). She was built in Italy in July 1981 but had been laid-up since the summer of 1983 over a dispute between her owners, the Castello Hellas Shipping Company, and builders. Sistership *Lucky Rider* had previously been sold to Stena Line at the close of 1984 for $3.2 million. The Swedes renamed her *Stena Driver* but she was purchased by Sealink in late 1985 and renamed *Seafreight Freeway*. A Fishguard crew was sent to collect her from Gothenburg but a disagreement on manning levels saw the vessel laid-up in the River Blackwater in Essex instead of deputising for the *St. Brendan*.

Folkestone: On 26th February, the *Horsa* ran aground in thick fog off Copt Point, Folkestone. All blades on both screws were bent and dry-docking at Chatham was required.

Following the loss of Calais sailings the previous June, all Ostend sailings were switched to Dover as from March thereby leaving Folkestone with the operation of the historic Boulogne link.

During October, the *Hengist* was required to operate the Fishguard–Rosslare route.

Both the *Hengist* and the *Horsa* received £1 million refits at Swan Hunter's yard during the winter months. The Orient Express Lounges were refurbished and new decor and seating were fitted throughout. The ships' after docking bridges were also removed during this period.

Newhaven: The start of the year saw the *Senlac* sail for the last time under the British flag. With Captain John Payne in command, she sailed as usual to Dieppe on the final day of January and defiantly played `Rule Britannia' over her tannoy as she entered the French port. Captain Payne called the occasion, "A sad day for the crew, a sad day for Newhaven and a sad day for Sealink British Ferries." After berthing at Newhaven for the final time under the British flag, the vessel destored and sailed to Le Havre for dry docking. S.N.C.F. took full control of the *Senlac* during late February and she was duly repainted in her new funnel colours and re-registered in Dieppe. The summer of 1985 was the first peacetime summer since 1825 that a British vessel had not plied from the Sussex Coast to Dieppe.

As from 1st February the service was due to be operated only by French ships but for the first nine days of the month the French crews were on strike fearing that there would be a cut in their manning levels. Eventually the dispute was resolved and the *Senlac* entered service on 27th February from Dieppe.

The planned three times a week Dieppe–Portsmouth freight service finally started on 9th March using the displaced Dunkerque based *Transcontainer I* with Brittany Ferries as their agents at the Hampshire port. Sadly the new link did not last long as with the impending Brittany Ferries link to Caen it was thought that the spheres of influence of the rival services would clash and so the Dieppe route was closed at the end of October.

The Newhaven–Dieppe service was maintained during 1985 with the *Senlac*, *Chartres* and *Cornouailles*.

Channel Islands: Channel Island Ferries started their rival ferry service to the Channel Islands on 3rd April using a sister ship to the *Earl Granville*, the *Corbiere*. The new company announced at the start of the year they were aiming to capture 20% of the market.

A national strike in Denmark delayed the completion at the Aalborg yard of the refit contract of the *Earl Granville* and *Earl William* for the end of March. The new 'Starliner' and 'Bateau de Luxe' service to Jersey and Guernsey had to be postponed and so the *Ailsa Princess* continued to run the old-style operation until the arrival of the newly converted vessels.

To commence the seasonal Weymouth–Cherbourg route, Sealink brought in the Rederi AB Gotland ferry *Thjelvar* (ex. *Gotland*) of 1964. At 2,900 gross tons and with a limited capacity, the ship opened the route on 1st April. The five week charter ended on 4th May, after which the spare R.M.T. unit *Prins Philippe* took up the route two days later. She was handed back to her owners at Ostend on 1st October. It had originally been planned to operate the *Manx Viking* (renamed *Earl Henry*) from the Heysham–Douglas route.

Sealink British Ferries' luxury overnight service to the Channel Islands finally became fully operational on 30th April, almost exactly a month late, when the *Earl Granville* arrived from Denmark to join the *Earl William* which had itself started the previous week running opposite the *Ailsa Princess*. The new operation boasted its own marketing team, brochure and fare structure which was inclusive of berth and meals. The overnight sailing from the Channel Islands sailed direct to Portsmouth as did the sailing from Portsmouth to the Islands. The daylight sailings from both destinations sailed, via Cherbourg. The new service was slow to attract the anticipated level of trade because of the very different fare structure and relatively high cost compared to that of the service from Weymouth by Sealink and the rival operation from Portsmouth which offered a relatively low fare structure.

Sealink British Ferries and Channel Island Ferries commenced a full scale price and marketing war once both operations became fully operational. By the end of June, Channel Island Ferries were claiming that they had captured 85% of the passenger traffic and 80% of the vehicle traffic between Portsmouth and the Islands. These claims were strongly disputed by Sealink British Ferries who maintained that their 'Starliner' service was aimed at a different sector of the market with their inclusive cabin and meals fare structure.

The daylight service to Cherbourg, marketed as the 'Bateau de Luxe' route, fared better than the company had

anticipated. The new 'Sunliner' service to the Channel Islands was also to exceed expectations with good loadings. The 'Sunliner' pattern of sailings, with both the *Ailsa Princess* (renamed *Earl Harold* during May)) and *Earl Godwin* lying overnight in the Channel Islands, was to prove more popular than the Portsmouth service, but the late evening arrivals of this service to both Islands were not liked by holidaymakers or hoteliers. By the end of the summer Martin Miller, the South-West Director of the company, was claiming that there was room for only one operator to and from the mainland to the Island.

Following a very successful season, Channel Island Ferries' vessel *Corbiere* was sent to Rotterdam for further improvements to her passenger areas for the forthcoming season. The Brittany Ferries' vessel *Cornouailles* stood in on the service in her absence. The very competitive and simple fare structure by Channel Island Ferries had not only seen off Sealink British Ferries but to some extent had attracted trade from the airlines. In an effort to attract even more trade to the route during the winter months, a new standby fare of £28 was introduced.

Another competitor ferry company, Torbay Seaways, announced that they would in 1986 operate their rival service to the Channel Islands, with the former West Highlands side-loading car ferry *Hebrides* from Caledonian MacBrayne. The vessel was renamed *Devoniun II* for her new role.

By the end of the summer Sealink British Ferries announced drastic measures in a bid to return the Channel Islands and Cherbourg services once again to a profitable operation. The Portsmouth-Channel Islands-Cherbourg routes continued with a two-ship operation but there were major reductions made by the company in the fare structure, with extras such as cabin accommodation once again available at supplementary rates. Meanwhile, the Weymouth–Jersey/Guernsey services were cut back to a single ship, the *Earl Godwin*, while the *Earl Harold* was switched back to the Irish Sea. The October announcement also sought about 250 voluntary redundancies to the Weymouth and Portsmouth work forces. The service to the Islands was to be marketed as British Ferries as from the next year, instead of Sealink British Ferries.

Irish Sea–Joint agreement with B&I: During early February 1985 Sealink British Ferries and B&I Line announced

Left: *The chartered Swedish vessel* **Felicity** *at Fishguard in November 1990 as the* **Stena Cambria** *arrives from Rosslare.* (Miles Cowsill)

Below: *The* **St. Christopher** *leaving Calais for Dover following the extension to her duty-free facilities at her after end.* (John Hendy)

*The Swedish ferry **Thjelvar** was chartered for the Weymouth-Cherbourg link in April 1985. (D. Hancox)*

*Seen at the Weymouth linkspan, R.M.T's **Prins Philippe** took over the Cherbourg link for the rest of the 1985 season. (David Parsons)*

that they had concluded discussions aimed at solving over-capacity on the Irish Sea. Talks had started during December against a background of achieving sailings for both rival companies on bringing frequency of service more in line with demand.

Certain reductions on the daylight sailings were made at Fishguard, whilst B&I Line's Rosslare–Pembroke Dock service was suspended during the company's overhaul programme and traffic was transferred to Fishguard under the agreement. Meanwhile, on 15th April, Sealink British Ferries acquired the *Stena Normandica* from Stena Line and shortly afterwards she was renamed *St. Brendan*.

In a further move, Sealink British Ferries announced more reductions in their operation on the Irish Sea in a revised agreement with B&I Line. The major change as far as the St. George's Channel services were concerned was the closure of the Rosslare–Pembroke Dock route with the loss of 535 jobs. Sealink British Ferries in return agreed to introduce "a new jumbo ferry" which was rumoured at the time to be T.T. Line's *Peter Pan*. In the event nothing came of these plans.

The pattern of sailings as far as Holyhead was concerned was to see the *St. Columba* and B&I sisters, *Leinster* and *Connacht*, operating alternately with the Danish-built ship.

Heysham: Early in the year, a formula was agreed between Sealink Manx Line and the Isle of Man Steam Packet Co. to merge their operations. Under the terms of the agreement, Sealink took a 40% holding in the Steam Packet and introduced the Stranraer ship *Antrim Princess* from 5th October while the Steam Packet provided the *Mona's Isle* (VI), the former Townsend Thoresen ferry *Free Enterprise III*. The latter proved to be an operational disaster and remained in service for less than six months before finishing in October and later being sold to Saudi Arabian interests.

◆ 1986

In a New Year's message to his employees, James Sherwood outlined more plans for the future of Sealink.

At Harwich the main problem concerned the *St. Nicholas* which the company had recently tried to purchase from Stena who demanded an exorbitant price. The bare-boat charter arranged under nationalised ownership was "unsatisfactory" and although this was extended until the summer of 1987, unless Stena dropped their price British Ferries would be looking for a vessel of more reasonable cost.

The former Harwich–Zeebrugge 'Sea Freightliner'

container vessels could well be switched to a Rotterdam or even to an inland German port although manning levels would have to be reduced. The Zeebrugge train ferry *Speedlink Vanguard* was to be returned to Stena during the summer after which all train ferry services would be based at Dover.

An agreement had been made with D.F.D.S. to start a new seasonal car ferry service linking an east coast U.K. port with Scandinavia as from spring 1987. The ship would be owned by Sealink although the Danes insisted that the catering staff should be supplied by them. The service would be a 50 -50 joint venture.

On the Tilbury–Gravesend ferry across the River Thames, no buyer had been found. The plan was to replace the *Edith* with a smaller vessel, slim the manning levels and persuade the local councils to subsidise the loss-making Sunday and holiday services. It was hoped to merge this service with those of another Thames operator.

At Dover both the *St. Anselm* and *St. Christopher* were further being improved to uprate their on-board sales. Mr. Sherwood wrote of a "conspiracy" involving the Belgian Transport Minister. The Belgians had stated that they were not denying access to British Ferries' ships, simply that there was no room at the berths or any standing space for freight. North Sea Ferries had offered British Ferries use of their new terminal at Zeebrugge but a new route from Dover had been given the "thumbs down" from the port authority there. Should British Ferries ever again start operating to Belgium then Zeebrugge would be the preferred port although the *St. David* would be too slow to operate twice daily and would probably be retained by Stranraer.

In the meantime, British Ferries were looking to the Dover–Dunkerque West route and the *Seafreight Freeway* (managing agreements permitting) was expected to appear on the service.

At Folkestone a new high speed service would be introduced in 1987 which would place a question mark over the future of the *Vortigern*.

Of the Channel Islands routes, Mr. Sherwood called it a "fiasco" and wrote of "dreadful circumstances" with British Ferries "fighting a battle for survival." Due to Brittany Ferries adding capacity on their Portsmouth–Caen and Poole–Cherbourg links, Mr. Sherwood foresaw a "bloodbath" on the Portsmouth–Cherbourg service. A pricing policy had been adopted to discourage Channel Islands Ferries from continuing with their rival service.

Fishguard–Rosslare had a successful 1985 and a larger ship was still being sought. The *St. Brendan* might be used on any future Dover–Belgium route or possibly traded in part-payment for the larger ship. The possibility of opening a new service from Fishguard to northern Spain in spring 1987 was being investigated. At Rosslare the port arrangements were "unsatisfactory" and Irish Railways "seem unprepared to respect our wishes concerning port operation."

At Holyhead the dry dock was to be sold but a deep water linkspan was under construction at Salt Island which would allow the *Seafreight Highway* to operate to Dublin. At this time the twin lo–lo vessels would be sold and the containers shipped via Stranraer.

On the Manx route, steam trains were proposed linking Lancaster and Heysham for all sailings, whilst at Stranraer British Ferries would not be averse to acquiring the Townsend Thoresen operation from European Ferries. The *St. Brendan* could be switched to the North Channel if the *St. David* was required elsewhere.

During June, Sea Containers purchased Hoverspeed for £5 million after which the craft all had 'British Ferries' added to their livery. The company stated that it was looking towards the introduction of wave-piercing catamarans and was 'not hopeful' that the hovercraft would continue in service.

Harwich: After the departure of the chartered *Zeeland* in March, S.M.Z. briefly chartered the spare Brittany Ferries vessel *Armorique*. The new £40 million ferry was named *Koningin Beatrix* (31,180 gross tons) on 9th November 1985 before entering service on 22nd April. James Sherwood announced the building of a similarly-sized vessel for entry into service in spring 1988.

The *Prinses Beatrix* passed to her French owners at the close of that month and serves today as their *Duc de Normandie*.

The Harwich–Zeebrugge lo–lo service had closed on 5th December 1985 after which the *Sea Freightliner I* and *Sea Freightliner II* were laid-up up Parkeston Quay. At the end of July the *Sea Freightliner I* was towed to the River Blackwater and was joined there by her sister on 1st August. In February 1987, the first ship sailed from Falmouth to Naples where she loaded electrical goods for China. Thereafter she was broken up at Kaohsiung in Taiwan. As for the *Sea Freightliner II*, during

ISLE OF WIGHT SERVICES

Top left: *The second of a trio of vessels built at Dundee for Sealink's Isle of Wight services in 1973, the* **Cenwulf** *leaves Yarmouth for Lymington. (John Hendy)*

Top right: *The* **St. Helen** *was the second of a quartet of car ferries built for the Portsmouth - Fishbourne (Isle of Wight) link. (John Hendy)*

Bottom left: *The Isle of Wight passenger ferry* **Southsea** *(Captain Bill Frampton) arriving at Ryde during her 1987 season of Solent cruises. After forty years of faithful service, the Denny-built vessel was finally retired the following September. (John Hendy)*

Bottom right: *The diesel passenger vessels were replaced on the Ryde ferry link during 1986 when a pair of Tasmanian-built catamarans took over the service. The second of the new twins,* **Our Lady Pamela,** *arrives at Ryde in August 1987. (John Hendy)*

*The Swedish ferry **Viking 4** was purchased during 1980 and took up the Portsmouth - Channel Islands service the following year as the **Earl Granville**. She is seen arriving at Portsmouth during August 1988. (Miles Cowsill)*

September 1986 she sailed to Naples where she loaded a cargo of pipes arriving at Karachi (Pakistan) for demolition in the New Year 1987.

Dover: The ending of the R.M.T./Sealink trading agreement as from 1st January caused major repercussions. James Sherwood stated that his company had lost over £1 million on the Ostend route in 1985, partly because the Belgians wouldn't give them a fair pool share and partly because the *St. David* had too many crews. Sherwood contacted Nicholas Ridley (Secretary of State for Transport) asking him to retaliate by using his powers to close British ports to all Belgian ferries until such time that the Belgian Government chose to allow Sealink British Ferries vessels back into Ostend or Zeebrugge. All Belgian vessels were prevented from using the Admiralty Pier linkspan which caused severe problems for all operators. Shut-out of Belgium, the company sought to expand operations through Dunkerque West with their recently purchased freight vessels *Seafreight Highway* and *Seafreight Freeway*. Strikes over manning levels prevented the new ships from entering service and so the *St. Anselm* (in the New Year) followed by the S.N.C.F. vessel *Transcontainer I* (in February) commenced

The **St. Brendan** *seen leaving Rosslare in the joint livery of B&I and Sealink. (Miles Cowsill)*

the new link to Dunkerque West. The 'Freeway' eventually started on 21st July.

The New Year also saw the end of the Sealink Dover–Boulogne route with the *Cote d'Azur* completing the final rites on the Saturday services.

As part of Sea Containers' policy of uprating and improving on-board facilities, the *St. Anselm* and *St. Christopher* were both sent to to Papenburg, West Germany during the early part of the year to undergo refits costing in the region of £1.5 million. The 'Anselm' returned to service on 14th March but delays with the 'Christopher' saw the *Vortigern* back on the Dover–Calais service.

During October, plans were drawn up to jumboise the *St. Anselm* and *St. Christopher* by inserting either a 50 ft. or 100 ft. section amidships and the same month again saw the *Vortigern* on the route vice the *St. Christopher* which went off service with crankshaft problems. The *Vortigern* finished on 17th November but was later about to be transferred to Weymouth. As it was, she remained in the Dover Strait to cover the winter refits of the *Hengist* and *Horsa*.

The former *Earl Siward* was purchased by the Quadrini Group early in the year and was eventually towed from Cyprus to the Tyne during March/April for conversion to leisure/night club use. As the *Tuxedo Royale*, the vessel is presently berthed at Gateshead. She replaced the former *Caledonian Princess* (renamed *Tuxedo Princess*) which was removed to Glasgow.

Folkestone: During the summer season, the *Vortigern* was rostered for just a single round crossing from Folkestone to Boulogne and completed her scheduled sailings on 27th September.

After Sea Containers acquired Hoverspeed in June, they stated that two of the smaller craft could be converted to passenger-only operation for the Folkestone–Boulogne link.

Newhaven: In late spring 1986, S.N.C.F. formed a subsidiary company, Dieppe Ferries, to manage the future of their Newhaven service. The service had been strike-ridden and required a new image and identity if it was to succeed. The new company stated that they wished to both enhance the quality of the service and also to upgrade the facilities on board their vessels. A start was made by building a new duty-free supermarket in the *Chartres*. S.N.C.F. also gave Dieppe

Ferries four years to turn the loss-making route into a profit.

The charter of the *Cornouailles* from Brittany Ferries finished in 1986. Her place was taken by the twenty year old Calais ferry *Chantilly* which underwent a £600,000 refit at Le Havre prior to taking up service on the route. Her forward bar area was extended by 12 ft. to house a supermarket, the roof of which provided a new forward for passengers. At the aft end the old bar area was extended, totally refitted and a small area was converted to a lorry drivers' restaurant. A new waiter-service restaurant was also provided as was a new general lounge and 350 reclining seats. The vessel took up service with the *Chartres* and *Senlac* during the early spring.

On 20th November Stena Line's *Stena Nautica* (ex. *Stena Danica*, ex. *Stena Nordica*) underwent berthing trials at Newhaven and later Dieppe. With passenger accommodation for as many as 1,800 and car capacity at two levels for 425, almost double that of the *Chartres* and *Senlac*, immediate charter terms were agreed by Dieppe Ferries for a two year period as from April 1987. It was decided that £750,000 should be spent on her accommodation, including a new Euro-lounge, a coffee shop and aircraft seating. A new internal ramp would also be fitted on the vehicle deck. The vessel had previously operated for R.M.T. on their Ostend–Dover link.

A newspaper competition involving the 'Daily Mirror' and a French paper was held to choose a name for Dieppe Ferries' new ship. Nearly 9,000 entries were eventually received, her pending arrival was seen as the start of an upturn in the route's affairs.

The name chosen for the vessel was the *Versailles*–a popular revival of a name carried by one of the previous ships on the route. In order to accommodate the new ferry, £1 million was spent at Newhaven on dredging and widening the harbour entrance by 12 metres with the removal of the old Eastern Pier.

Meanwhile, the *Chartres* was sent for a £750,000 overhaul.

Channel Islands: Following the October announcement the previous year, Sealink decided not to transfer the *Earl Harold* to the Irish Sea, but that she should maintain the Channel Islands service from Weymouth while the *Earl Godwin* would be employed on the seasonal service between Weymouth and Cherbourg.

Despite Sealink British Ferries' altered marketing strategy for their Portsmouth–Channel Islands route for 1986, rivals Channel Island Ferries were still claiming by the early summer that they were carrying more than half the traffic to Jersey and Guernsey with their single ship. Statistics for the first four months of the year from C.I.F. showed the *Corbiere* handling 53% of the passenger sea traffic with the remaining 47% split between the *Earl Granville* and *Earl William*.

In an effort to give further publicity to their Portsmouth-Cherbourg service, Champagne Mumm agreed a joint sponsorship challenge known as Cordon Rouge which was introduced to mark the fastest crossing by a passenger ship from Portsmouth, using the Nab Tower off the Isle of Wight as the start point, to the outer breakwater at Cherbourg. The distance of some 62 nautical miles was covered by the *Earl Granville* on 18th July in 3 hours 27 minutes. Amid a blaze of publicity and a huge red pennant streaming from her foremast, the vessel only operated somewhat faster than her usual timings. Ironically the press party who had travelled out on the *Earl Granville* on the trophy's premier challenge returned on the *Earl William*, which cut some 30 minutes off the 'Granville's' outward sailing.

In a joint statement on 30th September, Channel Island Ferries and Sealink British Ferries announced that they intended to join forces on the Channel Island services and to be known as British Channel Island Ferries (B.C.I.F.). Sealink's *Earl Granville* (the near sister to the *Corbiere*) would be retained to run with the *Corbiere* from Portsmouth. The *Earl William* would be withdrawn from the route along with the two Sealink ships at Weymouth. The Weymouth service in future would only operate during the summer with one of the former Sealink Weymouth vessels.

As a result of Sealink's announcement, and also for the way they implemented the merger, officers and crews of the four Sealink Channel Island vessels immediately took industrial action. A series of 'sit-ins' began on board the four ships, the *Earl William* at St. Peter Port, *Earl Godwin* at Weymouth, *Earl Granville* at Cherbourg and later the *Earl Harold* when she arrived at Portsmouth. Having been served by five ferries during the summer the Islands were left in the hands of one vessel–the *Corbiere*. She was able to cope with the autumn passenger traffic, but freight soon began to be a problem. At Guernsey, the *Earl William* had blocked the linkspan at St. Peter Port, so the *Corbiere* was not able to dock

Above: The **St. Nicholas** replaced both the **St. George** and **St. Edmund** on the Harwich - Hook of Holland service. She is seen at the commencement of her regular morning sailing as she sails down the River Stour en-route for Holland. (John Hendy)

Right: The Austrian-built **Darnia** arriving at Larne from Stranraer in August 1990. (John Hendy)

Below: During Sea Containers' period of Sealink ownership, twin Greek, deep-sea, ro-ro vessels were purchased for eventual use on the Dover - Zeebrugge and Dunkerque services. The **Seafreight Freeway** and **Seafreight Highway** were later sold in part-exchange for the vessels which became the **Fantasia** and **Fiesta**. (FotoFlite)

Above: After the closure of the Harwich and then the original Dover train ferry workings, the **Cambridge Ferry** was switched to the Fishguard station where she operated in a freight capacity. She is seen leaving Rosslare, Co. Wexford. (Miles Cowsill)

Left: The Harwich train ferry **Speedlink Vanguard** (ex. **Stena Shipper**) arriving at Dunkerque West in May 1986. (Miles Cowsill)

Bottom left: The former Manx Line vessel **Manx Viking** is seen arriving at Heysham from Douglas in July 1981. (D.I. Harmsworth)

Bottom right: The lo - lo vessel **Brian Boroime** sits under the container cranes at Holyhead in November 1989. (Miles Cowsill)

and Channel Island Ferries decided that they would have to unload cars and freight at St. Helier. Traffic for Guernsey was then transferred to Torbay Seaways vessel *Devoniun II*, which had a side loading ramp and did not have to use the linkspan at St. Peter Port. Passengers for Guernsey were taken by the *Corbiere* and disembarked at the nearby quay. The crew of the *Earl William* then prevented the *Corbiere* docking there and so passengers had to be transferred ashore by boat. Channel Island Ferries advised the port authorities at St. Peter Port that if they were prevented from docking on their next call to the Island, the service to Guernsey would be suspended. Nevertheless the *Corbiere* was prevented from docking on 13th October. Channel Island Ferries closed the service to Guernsey for five days and it was not until 18th October that the link was resumed, following agreement being reached for the *Corbiere* to use the linkspan once again. The *Earl William* sailed to Weymouth to join the rest of the Sealink fleet on strike.

After ten days a complex settlement was reached with the unions and the Sealink crews at the other ports returning to normal working. Sadly Sealink British Ferries were unable to reach agreement with the N.U.S. and N.U.M.A.S.T., the officers' union, to join the new venture and as a result of this they were unable to offer the *Earl Granville* and *Earl Harold* (for Weymouth) for the new service.

Channel Island Ferries then took out a series of high court injunctions against their Sealink partners, which they won. Under an interim agreement with Sealink, Channel Island Ferries was allowed to trade as B.C.I.F. Sealink also undertook not to offer any services to the Islands for twelve months.

B.C.I.F. rejected Sealink's offer of the *Vortigern* to maintain the Weymouth service and in the event chartered in the former P&O Normandy Ferries vessel *Lion*, which since her sale to Greek owners in 1985, had traded as the *Baroness M*. She was renamed *Portelet* during her Channel Islands stint.

Sealink/B&I: On the Irish Sea, Sealink had planned to tie in their refits at both Fishguard and Holyhead with their operating partners B&I. The Irish Company were faced with a further period of industrial disputes and Sealink were forced to revise their plans by bringing the *Vortigern* to Fishguard to cover for the refit of the *St. Brendan*.

The B&I ferry service between Rosslare and Pembroke Dock closed on Sunday, 5th January 1986 with the 02.15 service to Ireland. The closure of the link was a major blow to the economy and tourist trade of South Pembrokeshire and Ireland. Sealink made worldwide enquiries to find a large new jumbo ship to replace the *St. Brendan* but the company were unsuccessful. It was therefore decided that as a temporary measure for the 1986 season the *St. Brendan* would operate with the B&I vessel *Innisfallen*, which would undertake extra sailings to meet demand on the southern corridor during the peak season. Initially the *Innisfallen* could not be released as she was required elsewhere in the company's fleet and the Belgian ferry *Prins Philippe* was chartered from R.M.T. for three weeks prior to her arrival.

Sealink planned to withdraw the *St. Columba* for a five week period whilst she underwent an £80,000 internal refit on the Clyde in the early New Year. Her place was planned to be taken by the *Leinster* under the joint agreement between Sealink and B&I. However, the crew of the *Leinster* went on strike, which delayed the departure of the `Columba'. There was no sign of the industrial dispute being concluded so the 'Columba' was withdrawn for a short overhaul only until 14th April when the *St. David* was able to relieve her for her major refit in Germany. On 20th May the *St. Columba* returned to

*The **Versailles** arriving at Newhaven. (Miles Cowsill)*

*From right to left, the **Earl Godwin**, **Earl Harold** and **Earl William** strike bound at Weymouth. (Ferry Publications Library)*

her home port following her internal improvements, which included a Pullman Lounge and new restaurant.

The *St. David* then sailed north to operate on the Stranraer-Larne service with the *Galloway Princess* and *Darnia*.

Under the terms of the joint arrangement, B&I and the Irish Government approved similar internal improvements to the *Leinster* and *Connacht* to bring them up to the standard of the Sealink British Ferries operation. Meanwhile, on the Irish Sea, Sealink and B&I agreed that their joint operation should be marketed as Southern Seaways.

Heysham: The *Manx Viking* was duly painted in Isle of Man Steam Packet colours during January but was finally withdrawn from service on 29th September. She was sold the following March to operate a service across Stavanger Fjord as the *Skudenes* but in March 1989 she sailed to Lake Huron in Canada where as the *Nindawayama* she operated for Ontario Northland Marine Services between Tobermory and Manitoulin Island.

Stranraer: Over one million passengers were carried on the Stranraer-Larne service during 1986 and the number of vehicles carried on the route increased by some 10%.

Mediterranean: Under the command of Captain Brian Hills, Sea Containers duly introduced their French-built, Finnish ferry *Orient Express* (ex. *Silja Star*) to operate their new service from Venice - Piraeus–Kusadasi–Patmos–Katakleon–Venice on 3rd May, leaving Venice every Saturday and making one round trip in every 6½ days. The vessel was built in 1975 and was of 12,343 gross tons. The *Orient Express* sailings were scheduled to link with the train of that name which operated from Boulogne to Venice. The service ended in 1989.

◆ 1987

Harwich: During January, the D.F.D.S. ferry *Dana Anglia* was briefly chartered to cover the services of both regular vessels on the Hook link.

The Harwich–Zeebrugge train ferry service was terminated on 31st January after which the *Cambridge Ferry* was transferred to Dover while the *Speedlink Vanguard* was returned to Stena Line.

The 'Cambridge' in fact operated her final sailing on Christmas Eve before departing to Immingham for refit on 29th December 1986.

Sea Containers announced during the year that they were investigating a new route linking Harwich with Kiel.

Dover: The *Cambridge Ferry* duly carried out berthing trials at Dover's train ferry dock on 2nd February but did not enter service until 16th March. On 1st May she was involved in a collision with the *Saint Eloi* 700 yards off Dover Breakwater as a result of which both vessels were badly damaged.

The Belgian threat weakened when in April the Port of Zeebrugge Authority allowed Sealink British Ferries to operate a service from Dover.

After having left Marseilles after a £750,000 refit on 14th May, the *Seafreight Highway* entered service from Dover on 20th May and the Zeebrugge link finally commenced on 23rd June with the 'Highway' making the initial crossing. Sealink were now able to offer two daily return services from the Western Docks in addition to two daily return sailings to Dunkerque West from the Eastern Docks.

The 'new' ships were to prove far from ideal being deep-sea vessels in which fast turn rounds were not essential yet this attribute was vital if they were to be successful as short-

Above: The first of the two former Bulgarian ro-ro freighters purchased by Sea Containers was the **Channel Seaway** which, after operating in a freight mode from Dover to Calais during summer 1989, was sent to Bremerhaven from where she later emerged as the **Fiesta**. (John Hendy)
Right: The Lloyd Werft yard at Bremerhaven sees the **Channel Seaway** on the left and the **Fiesta** under conversion in the Kaiserdok. The ship became Sealink's **Fantasia**. (John Hendy)
Below: In service at Calais, the **Fantasia** as she originally appeared with non-standard yellow line around her hull, dark blue trading name and full length funnel markings. (John Hendy)

sea traders. As it was, a 2 hours 30 minutes turn round was far too long and in order to keep to tight schedules in port, the ships rarely sailed full once hour turnrounds were rostered. They were difficult to handle and their high-revving engines were the cause for many concerns. Their lack of speed prevented them from operating a double round sailing to Zeebrugge each day which, claimed Sherwood, was imperative if the route was to be a commercial success.

Following the tragedy off Zeebrugge in March 1987, from 1st April Townsend Thoresen duly chartered the spare *Vortigern* for £250,000 over a period of 60 days for use on their Dover–Boulogne link. With this completed on 1st June, she sailed to the Fal to lay-up.

During the morning of 16th October, hurricane gusts battered the south east of England and the *St. Christopher*, which had gone to the Downs (off Deal) to shelter was hit by seas of such force that the steel door on her upper vehicle deck below the bridge was split open and some cargo overturned. The vessel later berthed at Dover and her sailings were taken by the *Horsa* which was unable to use Folkestone due to damage to the station and port.

The *Seafreight Highway* was in collision with the cafe at the end of the Prince of Wales' Pier that same night and large pieces of its structure were bounced across the harbour and thrown onto the Eastern Arm. With the new train ferry berth on the Admiralty Pier badly damaged by the hurricane, the *Cambridge Ferry* and the *Saint-Germain* were retained in service longer than anticipated.

Folkestone: Worse was to befall the *Hengist* which was alongside at Folkestone when the storm started. With lines constantly snapping as a result of the huge swells along the pier, she was forced to put to sea and just off the port was hit by a wave of such force that falling machinery caused alternator damage after which all electrical power in the ship was lost. With the engines unable to restart, Captain Sid Bridgewater called all crew to the bridge where lines were laid out. The south westerly winds, blowing to hurricane force, were driving the stricken *Hengist* onto the Warren (the beach between Dover and Folkestone at the base of the chalk cliffs) and there were fears that the ship would roll over once she had grounded. Fortunately the *Hengist* was impaled by a concrete knuckle of sea wall which was driven over half way through her engine room. The ship became something of a

The French built ferry **Orient Express** *is seen here en-route to Venice prior to entering service. (FotoFlite)*

celebrity and was finally rescued on 22nd October not re-entering service until the following January. The *Vortigern* (without an operational bow rudder or bow thrust unit) was recalled from the Fal to deputise during the *Hengist's* absence.

Newhaven: The *Chantilly* and *Senlac* were withdrawn from service on the Newhaven–Dieppe link once the *Versailles* and *Chartres* had completed their extensive modifications to the service. The *Chantilly* was sold to Greek interests and renamed *Olympia*. The *Senlac* meanwhile was to be chartered for the forthcoming summer by B&I Line on their Fishguard-Rosslare link. Dieppe Ferries then chartered an additional ferry for the route, the dedicated Canadian roll on-roll off *Marine Evangeline* (ex. *Duke of Yorkshire*) but the vessel was to prove totally unsuitable for the route. The *Versailles* finally entered service on 19th April and shortly afterwards the company were claiming that the *Chartres* would also need to be replaced by a larger and more suitable running partner for the new vessel. The new ship was to experience a series of engine problems starting in August and with the *Senlac* on charter, the *Saint Eloi* had to be brought into cover from the Dunkerque–Dover train ferry service. Later the *Vortigern* was brought in to cover for the vessel (as from 6th August) and on completion of the *Senlac's* charter to B&I at the end of September she was once again on the route. The vessel that had been promoted as "the Palace by name–Palace by nature", continued to experience further engine problems which were to cause disruptions and delays to passengers on the link. During bad weather the vessel was also unable to maintain the scheduled crossing times.

The *Senlac* was sold by Dieppe Ferries later in the year to Ventouris Coast Lines of Greece and serves today as the *Apollo Express I*.

South West: The *Earl Granville* which had been laid up in Portsmouth since October following the strike the previous season, returned to operation on 15th April reopening the Portsmouth–Cherbourg service. Meanwhile the *Earl Harold* was employed on the Weymouth-Cherbourg service. The *Earl William* remained at Weymouth during the winter and it was rumoured by the early spring that Sealink had entered negotiations with the Home Office to use the vessel as a immigration detention centre for refugees and visitors refused entry to Britain. Negotiations were finally concluded with the Government and the vessel arrived at the old Harwich train ferry dock during the second week of May to start another stage of her lengthy career. Some 120 detainees were housed on the ship initially. Meanwhile a specialist security company was employed to look after them as members of the N.U.S. were opposed to working on what they termed, "a prison ship."

Some of the worst storms for 500 years struck southern England during the early hours of Friday 16th October. The *Earl William*, with more than 40 Tamil refugees on board, broke away from her moorings and drifted across Harwich harbour towards the mouth of the River Stour for around two hours until an anchor could be dropped. Her reluctant guests were later taken off and given temporary permission to stay in Britain.

Fishguard: The spare *Vortigern* was called to operate the Fishguard–Rosslare route during mid-January while the *St. Brendan* was on overhaul before completing her service on 4th February.

B&I chartered the French ferry *Senlac* from Dieppe Ferries as a second back-up vessel to the *St. Brendan* on the Fishguard-Rosslare service in 1987. She took up service on 18th June until September. The winter refit of the *St. Brendan* saw the vessel going to the Mersey for overhaul with the *St. David* from Stranraer deputising for her absence. While the *St. Brendan* was away on refit she received a one-off livery incorporating the logos of both Sealink and B&I Line.

A further four vessels assisted at Fishguard during 1987. The *Darnia* deputised in May, when she was sent to the port to cover for engine problems with the *St. Brendan* and during August the *Stena Sailer* was sent to back-up the route at the height of the peak season. October saw the Weymouth-based *Earl Harold* being transferred to cover for the absence of the 'Brendan' when she had to be withdrawn for further engine repairs. By late autumn the level of freight on the Southern Corridor had increased to such a level, that the company decided that an additional vessel would have to be brought in to support the *St. Brendan* during the lead up to Christmas. The veteran train ferry *Cambridge Ferry* was brought up from the Fal from lay-up after service at Dover.

Holyhead: At Holyhead the *St. David* once again relieved the *St. Columba* during her overhaul period from 27th February to 12th March. Meanwhile the *Earl Harold* was sent to the North Channel to cover for the refits of the *St. David*, *Galloway Princess* and *Darnia*.

Meanwhile, the *Stena Sailer* started supplementary sailings on the Holyhead-Dun Laoghaire service to support the *St. Columba*. B&I tried to obtain a High Court injunction halting the new specialist freight service during April.

During the early autumn B&I Line were facing major financial problems and the company was forced to look for further rationalisations in their services together with staff cuts. It was becoming more evident that the company would have to concentrate their efforts on the shorter Dublin–Holyhead service rather than the Liverpool route which was becoming less popular and more expensive to operate.

At the end of 1987 B&I withdrew from the pooling agreement with Sealink. As a result of their decision, the Irish company returned to their U.K. port of Pembroke Dock.

◆ 1988

Harwich: S.M.Z. was 70% state owned but in 1988 it was announced that the Dutch Government was to sell its interest in the company. Four prospective purchasers entered the race to purchase S.M.Z. : Sealink British Ferries, Nedlloyd, Johnson Line and Stena Line.

Dover: The port's original train ferry berth was finally closed on 16th May although the elderly French train ferry *Saint-Germain* carried her final trains on 8th May. The new French train ferry *Nord Pas-de-Calais* took up service from the new berth at No. 5 on the Admiralty Pier on 9th May but the *Cambridge Ferry* and the *Chartres* were brought back at the close of September until 13th October after the new berth had failed. During the 'NPC's' overhaul between 28th–30th December, the old dock was reactivated for a final time.

The train ferry *Saint Eloi* ended her association with the Dunkerque West link on 24th April after which she was painted all white and received major internal refurbishment before taking up service from Calais to Dover Western Docks on 27th May. Now on charter to S.N.C.F., and with a Calais crew, she operated the twice daily train connected services linking London (Victoria) and Paris (Gare du Nord). On 23rd July she received a badly dented stem when leaving the Admiralty Pier at Dover she was in collision with the pier at the western side of the old train ferry dock.

Unprecedented industrial unrest which involved the three month lay-up of all non-Sealink ships on the Dover–Calais route saw Sealink introduce the chartered Stena Line ferry *Scandinavica* (9,017 gross tons, built 1974) from 7th June. A night time freight run to Zeebrugge was included in her schedules but the route was becoming a drain on finances and it was no surprise when it was closed on 16th September with reported losses in excess of £1 million.

South West: Pressure from the travel trade and those connected with tourism on Guernsey persuaded Sealink to offer a twice a week service to St. Peter Port from Portsmouth via Cherbourg. When serving Guernsey the *Earl Granville* sailed overnight from Portsmouth with a Cherbourg call at 07.15 and an arrival at St. Peter Port at 10.00.

Meanwhile the Weymouth-based *Earl Harold*, which had completed her previous season on the Weymouth service,

was sent north once again just before the end of the year to relieve at Stranraer. After spending some seventeen months laid up on the River Fal, Sealink's *Earl Godwin* re-entered service on 17th March between Weymouth and Cherbourg. Following the arrival of the *Earl Harold*, the 'Godwin' moved to Portsmouth to maintain the additional sailings on the Portsmouth link with the *Earl Granville*.

After the announcement by B.C.I.F. that they intended to move their passenger operations from Portsmouth to Poole, there were calls from both Jersey and Guernsey for Sealink to return to the Islands with a fully fledged service from Portsmouth. No such service was ever to materialise, however the company did eventually market a freight ferry service from Portsmouth to the Islands for M.M.D. (Mainland Marketing Deliveries).

Holyhead: The *Vortigern* ended her career with Sealink when she was called in to assist with freight on the Dun Laoghaire route during March. After her final sailing on the last day of the month, she sailed the following day to Greece as the *Milos Express*.

At the beginning of August, the large *Seafreight Highway* appeared on the Holyhead–Dun Laoghaire run from Dover to support the *St. Columba*, which in turn allowed the *Stena*

*The **Hengist** aground in the Warren after the Great Storm of October 1987. (John Hendy)*

Sailer to be moved to the Fishguard-Rosslare route.

Following the entry into service of the *Seafreight Highway*, plans were drawn up for a stretched *Saint Eloi* to replace her. In the event the *Stena Sailer* replaced the large freight vessel which had proved totally unsuitable. The 'Highway' was sent to the River Fal to lay up with her sister vessel the *Seafreight Freeway* which had earlier closed the Dover–Zeebrugge freight service on 16th September. The *Stena Sailer* was later purchased by Sealink.

Liverpool: In the early New Year the Irish Government approved a restructuring plan for B&I Line agreeing to the closure of the Dublin–Liverpool service and to allow B&I to concentrate their sailings on the Central Corridor to Holyhead. Following this announcement, Sealink confirmed that they were considering establishing their own service from Liverpool to Dun Laoghaire in place of the B&I link. The company entered manning level discussions with the N.U.S. during early January to use the *Earl William* on the route. The feasibility study continued by the company despite B&I still claiming that they might possibly run a summer Dublin–Liverpool service. The *Earl William*, which commenced service on 25th April, was ideally appointed for

*Stena Line's **Stena Sailer** was on charter at Holyhead during 1987. (Ferry Publications Library)*

the new link with her well appointed cabins. Passenger numbers were limited to 600, which allowed most to acquire a berth for the overnight sailing. The service was slow to pick up but by the early summer bookings were showing encouraging signs.

Sadly, the route was suspended from 11th August after the *Earl William* developed problems with both her variable pitch propellers, one seizing completely and the other requiring attention. The 'William' was sent to Cardiff for dry docking, where initially it was thought the repairs would only take a week. The vessel reopened the service again on 24th August.

It was becoming evident by the early autumn that the Liverpool-Dun Laoghaire route was not attracting the business as anticipated. The engine problems at the height of the summer were to cause major losses for the company and there was reluctance by staff at Holyhead to support the service from Liverpool. Despite the early losses, it was decided that the route would continue. The *Earl Granville* was sent to Liverpool in November to cover for the absence of the *Earl William* whilst on refit but the former Channel Islands vessel was to prove totally unsuitable for the route.

◆ 1989

During early March, Stena Line AB of Gothenburg, Sweden, purchased 8% of Sea Containers' shares and Stena's Chief Executive announced that if proposed talks with James Sherwood failed then he would call on finances to launch an outright take-over of Sea Containers. The initial 8% was intended to be a "warning flag" of his intentions. Sherwood hoped that by gaining a Scandinavian ally, he could fight for a larger share of the market but in an increasingly competitive Scandinavia, Stena were now looking to extend their sphere of operations southwards. The year 1989 was marked by growing unrest and a rearguard action by Sea Containers to save itself from the advances of Tiphook (who sought their container business) and Stena who wished to absorb the Sealink ferry trade.

Harwich: To cover the refit of the *St. Nicholas* during January, Sealink transferred the Channel Islands vessel *Earl Granville* while her ro–ro traffic was transported by the *Mercandian Universe*. During the *Koningin Beatrix's* refit, the

The **Earl Harold** at Fishguard in October 1988. (Miles Cowsill)

The Stena Line vessel **Scandinavica** *was chartered at Dover for the 1988 season. (Ferry Publications Library)*

newly purchased Brittany Ferries' vessel *Duchesse Anne* maintained the service. To stave off the Stena Line approaches the *St. Nicholas* was sold for about £37 million during December to Gotland Rederi and leased back over five years with an option for another two.

Stena Line took over the ownership of S.M.Z. on 22nd June while on the final day of August, the *Koningin Beatrix* raised the Stena houseflag for the first time.

This was not an easy period for the route with Stena Line and Sealink British Ferries increasingly at loggerheads as the Swedes turned their interest on the Bahamian company. Such was the antagonism, that at one time Stena contemplated operating their service from Tilbury whilst Sealink looked to Europoort as their Dutch base. Stena gave Sealink 18 months' notice of their intention to end the pooling agreement as from February 1991.

Dover: The ro–ro vessel *Channel Seaway* entered service on the Dover–Calais link on 7th May. She was one of three sister ships built by Kockums of Malmo for AB Nordo Line and their freight operations to the eastern Mediterranean. The lead vessel *Zenobia* entered service in November 1979 but was lost eight months later following her cargo shifting

in heavy weather outside Larnaca Harbour, Cyprus. The other two ships of the series were launched as *Scandinavia* and *Ariadne* although a year later they were sold to the Bulgarian Government subsidiary, S.M.A.T. for whom they operated as the *Trapezitza* and *Tzarevetz*. Sea Containers purchased both vessels for about £30 million in part exchange for the unsuccessful *Seafreight Highway* and *Seafreight Freeway* in order to lead their crusade against the Channel Tunnel and to compete against P&O European Ferries' new 'Chunnel Beaters.'

The original plan was to convert both vessels for the Dover-Calais service for operations in 1989 vice the *St. Anselm* (to Fishguard) and the *St. Christopher* (to Newhaven). It was estimated that the conversion of the sisters was between 50–60% of the cost of newbuilding investment.

The first of the new sisters was hastily added to the Dover link, where she operated as the *Channel Seaway*, whilst the second was renamed *Fiesta* and went on charter to OT Africa Line.

The *Fiesta* was sent to Lloyd Werft for conversion in July where she became the Sealink British Ferries vessel *Fantasia* while the *Channel Seaway* followed in mid-October and eventually became S.N.C.F.'s *Fiesta*.

The **Vortigern** *arriving at Boulogne during September 1986. (John Hendy)*

After her unsuccessful Irish Sea exploits, the *Saint Eloi* was sent to Falmouth to refit and appeared at Calais on 20th May as the *Channel Entente*. After a further summer season on the train connected Calais–Dover Western Docks service, she was viewed by the Isle of Man Steam Packet Company who eventually purchased her for their Heysham/Liverpool–Douglas services on 14th February 1990. She remains in service as the *King Orry*.

The *Tynwald* (ex. *Antrim Princess*) made her final crossing to Heysham on 18th February prior to lay-up in the Fal. Sold to Italian owners Agostino Lauro, as the *Lauro Express* she left for Naples at the end of May 1990.

The spare Irish Ferries vessel *Saint Patrick II* was on charter to Sealink during the winter of 1989-90. She started in November on a daily double freight sailing to Calais.

South West: Following the move of B.C.I.F. from Portsmouth to Poole, the *Earl Godwin* opened a new freight link on 3rd January from Portsmouth to Jersey and Guernsey for M.M.D. and Commodore Shipping. The new route was designed to handle freight traffic previously carried through Portsmouth by B.C.I.F. It had originally been planned that the *Earl Granville* would undertake the new service but she was required at Harwich for the refit of the *St. Nicholas*.

As a result of the *Earl Harold's* charter to B&I, the *Earl Godwin* maintained the Weymouth–Cherbourg service in her place while the *Earl Granville* covered the Portsmouth–Cherbourg link. Meanwhile Sealink continued to manage the Portsmouth–Channel Islands services for M.M.D./Commodore Ferries using the *Earl Godwin* and *Earl Granville* until March, when the *Mads Mols* took over the route as a dedicated freight ship. The vessel was later renamed *Pride of Portsmouth*.

With the *Earl Granville* involved in a serious accident off Cherbourg on 19th August in which she tore a 15 metre gash in her hull and ruptured all tanks in her double bottom, the Isle of Man Steam Packet Co's side loading car ferry *Mona's Queen* took up charter sailings on the Portsmouth–Cherbourg route on 4th September. Irish Ferries' *Saint Patrick II* took over as from 15th September but the *Mona's Queen* was suddenly required at Weymouth over the weekend of 16th-17th September after the *Earl Godwin* had put back to port with engine problems. The Manx vessel left Weymouth for Douglas on 24th September.

Meanwhile, B&I handed back the former Stranraer vessel *Earl Harold* to Sealink at the end of October. She was later sold to Greek interests and renamed *Dimitri* then *Naias Express*.

Fishguard: Sealink and B&I entered negotiations during early January for the charter of the *Earl Harold* to the Irish company following the sale of the company's flagship vessel the *Connacht* to Brittany Ferries. The Sealink vessel was sent for a major overhaul prior to being chartered by B&I for their Rosslare-Pembroke Dock service. She appeared in full B&I livery during her charter period.

On 4th September Sealink British Ferries finally announced that they had secured a five-year charter as from March 1990 of the 15,001 gross ton ferry *Visby*. Negotiations had been going on for some time, and in fact the company had attempted to purchase the nine year old vessel throughout. The charter of the vessel with capacity for 1,600 passengers, 517 cars or 54 freight units, clearly showed the company's competitors that they were committed to the Southern Corridor by introducing the largest ever ship on the Irish Sea.

Holyhead: Following her service at Stranraer, the *Saint Eloi* then transferred to the Holyhead–Dun Laoghaire service in place of the *St. Columba* from 3rd-28th April. It was not a happy period of her career and resulted in many complaints from the travelling public.

Sealink closed the dedicated container service to Dublin as from 21st December. The two container vessels *Brian Boroime* and *Rhodri Mawr* were disposed of as part of the financial package against the Stena/Tiphook takeover bid. They were eventually sold to the Greek Sarlis Group and left as the *Peltainer* and *Peliner*. Following this announcement, Sealink confirmed that for the 1990 season they would introduce additional passenger sailings between Holyhead and Dun Laoghaire using the *Horsa* from Folkestone.

Stranraer: The former train ferry *Saint Eloi* made her debut on the Stranraer–Larne service between 8th January and 2nd April for the annual overhauls of the *Galloway Princess*, *Darnia* and *St. David*.

The **Earl William** *pictured in the Mersey with the Liver Building in the background. (Ferry Publications Library)*

◆ 1990

In April the hostile takeover battle for the control of Sea Containers was finally resolved. Most of the company's container business went to Tiphook for £321 million while Sealink British Ferries was acquired by Stena Line of Sweden for £259 million. As part of the deal Sea Containers retained the ports of Heysham, Newhaven and Folkestone plus the land development at Harwich. The lucrative Isle of Wight services, Hoverspeed and their holding in the Isle of Man Steam Packet Company were also retained by Sea Containers.

Stena Line immediately began a thorough re-evaluation of all ships and routes. The most outward sign of change was the adoption of the trading name Sealink Stena Line while the ships of the fleet eventually gained the 'Stena' prefix.

Harwich: One of the first moves made by Stena was to introduce the freighter *Stena Seatrader* onto the route as from 2nd May. Originally built as the train ferry *Svealand* in 1973, the vessel allowed both passenger ships to concentrate on the car accompanied traffic.

Dover/Folkestone: With the expected arrival of the new *Fantasia* from her conversion at Bremerhaven, the *St. Anselm* was duly transferred to the Folkestone–Boulogne route to run in tandem with the *Hengist* as from 11th February. Sister ship *Horsa* was sent to operate as the second Holyhead–Dun

*The **Felicity** and **St. Brendan** pass each other in the harbour entrance at Fishguard. (Miles Cowsill)*

Laoghaire vessel and arrived in the Welsh port on 5th March.

The new *Fantasia* (Captain Barry Thompson) arrived at Dover on 8th March and entered freight service to Calais on 11th March. Her first passenger sailing was six days later.

The French ferries were duly transferred from the ownership of S.N.C.F. Armement Naval to the Societe Propietaire des Navires (S.P.N.) on 22nd January. A further new company, Societe Navale Armement Transmanche (S.N.A.T.) was formed to operate the vessels. Their *Fiesta* arrived at Calais on 13th May and entered service, again as a freighter, on 22nd before taking up full service on 29th May. In preparation for her arrival, the *Champs Elysees* transferred to the Dieppe station, releasing the *Chartres* which became the seasonal Calais–Dover Western Docks train connected vessel as from 4th June. At one time it looked as if the Belgian ferry *Prince Laurent* (then on charter to S.N.A.T. at Dieppe) would open the seasonal route.

The *Chartres* was on charter to Sealink U.K.'s French subsidiary A.L.A. and carried their distinctive funnel markings for the rest of her period in service.

With the *Fantasia* requiring a quick return to Bremerhaven for attention to her new bow-thrust unit, the *Chartres* took up

a multi-purpose mode as from 3rd June and local Sealink management looked for the return of the *Horsa* from Holyhead. Instead they received the much-travelled *Earl William* which had recently returned to Milford Haven lay-up after a Belfast Car Ferries charter. The 'William' arrived at Dover on 3rd June and took up service from Folkestone to Boulogne three days later releasing the *St. Anselm* which transferred to Dover–Calais. After two days, the 'William's' hydraulic stern door failed and thereafter she operated as a passenger ship until 12th June. On that day the *Fantasia* took up service again and all returned to normal but later that month S.N.A.T. crews went on strike and closed Calais. The *Fantasia* operated a number of successful non-landing cruises to Calais while the *Chartres* operated to Boulogne and from 24th- 30th June to Zeebrugge.

The *St. Anselm* finished at Folkestone following a fire in her alternator room on 19th September after which she was sent to A&P Appledore at Wallsend for repair. The *Chartres* was sent to deputise on 30th September following the closure of her seasonal Calais–Dover Western Docks route. The *Horsa* reappeared on 15th October while the *Fantasia* went off service with a stuck bow-visor on 2nd December to be replaced by the *Stena Cambria* (ex. *St. Anselm*) fresh from refit at Wallsend.

South West: Following the *Earl Godwin* closing the Portsmouth–Cherbourg service for Sealink in December 1989, she then covered for the refit of the freighter *Pride of Portsmouth* on the M.M.D. Channel Islands freight service. Major engine problems were to be encountered on the *Earl Godwin* in her final days of service and repair work started during early February. However, in March the vessel was sold to Navarma Line. The Italian company bought the ship with the engine problem for some £2 million and renamed her *Moby Baby*.

As part of Stena Line's reorganisation of Sealink, it was announced that they would establish a new ferry service between Southampton and Cherbourg using the *St. Nicholas* from Harwich, which would be renamed *Stena Normandy*.

Fishguard: On 2nd March the giant *Felicity* arrived at Rosslare from Dunkerque for berthing trials before sailing to Fishguard. The Swedish ship had undergone a £2 million refit at Tilbury during the early New Year and it had been planned to put the vessel into service earlier. However an industrial dispute over manning levels failed to reached agreement and the vessel had to be laid up in Dunkerque.

The *Felicity* took up service on Monday 5th March with the 15.00 sailing to Rosslare. Meanwhile, the *St. Brendan* undertook her last official sailing for the company from Rosslare to Fishguard the previous evening. The *St. Brendan* was also sold to Navarma Line and was renamed *Moby Vincent*.

The *Cambridge Ferry* was sent to Milford Haven again for lay-up as she was not required at Fishguard due partly to a drop in trade on the Southern Corridor and the port did not require her as the *Felicity* offered adequate freight capacity. An upturn in traffic saw the veteran train ferry return to service again in late June until September.

Following the takeover of Sealink by Stena Line, it was announced in the autumn that the company would invest something in the region of £4.5 million in the Port of Fishguard over the next couple of years. Improvements would be made to the port facilities to enable the renamed *Stena Felicity* to turn round more quickly and to operate triple sailings each day as from 1992. The planned improvements

were to take place but the triple sailings at the peak of the season were never established.

The *Cambridge Ferry* saw service again over Christmas when passenger bookings exceeded all expectations and freight had to be transferred to her. On 27th December the *Stena Felicity* carried 516 cars on the 15.00 sailing to Rosslare–a port and company record for Sealink. The *Cambridge Ferry* retired once more in early January 1991 for a short period before being required again, but this time at Stranraer.

Holyhead: On the last day of January, a serious engine room fire broke out in the *St. Columba*. The vessel departed from Dun Laoghaire at 08.45 to Anglesey but about ten miles out was forced to drop anchor after fire was found in the port engine. Captain Bakewell issued a general May Day and fire fighting teams were sent by helicopter to assist. The fire was eventually put out in force 8 conditions and with the wind strengthening, two tugs were called to assist the vessel into Holyhead and she finally arrived in her home port at 21.00. The *St. Columba* was sent to Liverpool for repairs following the incident and the *Darnia* was sent from Stranraer to reopen passenger sailings before the Isle of Man Steam Packet Company's *Lady of Mann* was chartered in her place. The Folkestone vessel *Horsa* arrived at Holyhead on 5th March to replace the *Lady of Mann* and some two weeks later the *St. Columba* arrived back following repairs.

On 23rd May the *Horsa* took up her planned summer schedule on the Holyhead–Dun Laoghaire service until 4th September.

On 5th September the *St. Columba* was involved in a further unfortunate incident when she suffered main bearing failure to one of her engines. She was to remain out of service for over a month, her place being taken by the smaller *Horsa*.

Meanwhile at Holyhead, Stena Line unveiled an investment package for the Anglesey port. The new owners announced that the *St. Columba* would undergo a major £6 million refit which would include a complete rebuilding programme of all her passenger accommodation for the following season. The twelve year old ship would also be renamed *Stena Hibernia* following these works. To increase freight capacity on the link, the *St. Anselm/Stena Cambria* would be transferred from Folkestone to Holyhead to offer two additional round sailings a day. With a major investment by Sealink Stena Line in both Fishguard and Holyhead, B&I soon became very much a secondary operator on the Irish Sea, especially at Holyhead. The Government-owned company's hands were tied, having very little money to expand and improve their services. Meanwhile, B&I was put up for sale by the Irish Government and was later sold to Irish Ferries.

Liverpool: Further bad news hit the Irish Sea when it was announced that the Liverpool-Dun Laoghaire service would close as from 9th January with a loss of 100 jobs. The *Earl William* completed her last sailing between Ireland and Britain as scheduled and was then sent to Milford Haven for lay-up with the *Cambridge Ferry*. The former `Starliner' vessel however was back in service again on 28th January when she was chartered by Belfast Car Ferries following their vessel having to be withdrawn from service. She remained in service until March and once again was sent to Pembrokeshire for lay-up.

Stranraer: Following the fire on the *St. Columba*, refits at Stranraer were delayed. In a surprise move on 4th March in an effort to finish refits early on the North Channel, the redundant *Earl Granville* was sent to Stranraer to cover for overhauls of the *Galloway Princess* and *Darnia*. The

`Granville' proved a totally unsuitable ship on the link and the *Cambridge Ferry* was brought into service to support her. Following her short spell at Stranraer and the takeover of Sealink by Stena Line, she transferred to the Sea Containers' fleet. She was only to see a short period of service again in U.K. waters when she had to be called upon to operate Hoverspeed's new SeaCat service between Portsmouth and Cherbourg, following the delay of *Hoverspeed Great Britain* into service.

Major changes were also to take place at Stranraer. It was announced that the *St. Christopher* would be transferred from Dover and renamed *Stena Antrim* as from 1991. She would operate with the renamed *Stena Galloway* (ex. *Galloway Princess*) and *Stena Caledonia* (ex. *St. David*). As a result of the transfer of the *St. Christopher* to the Scottish port, the *Darnia* was to be sold.

◆ **1991**

Following a disastrous first year's trading, during which time Stena made a pre-tax loss of £28.2 million, Sealink Stena Line's Managing Director Gareth Cooper wrote to his employees, "I must express to you the seriousness of the company's position."

It was accepted within the industry that Stena's desire to

The **Horsa** leaving Dun Laoghaire for Holyhead. (Miles Cowsill)

The **St. Anselm** was switched to the Folkestone service during 1990. (John Hendy)

The **Stena Fantasia** (left) and the French **Fiesta** at Calais in 1991. (John Hendy)

acquire the ferry operations of Sea Containers had resulted in an offer in excess of the company's market value and that severe retrenchments were now necessary. It was believed that Sealink was worth in the region of £180 million and yet Stena had paid £259 million, had immediately invested a further £178 million in new ships, opened a new route between Southampton and Cherbourg and taken on £200 million of Sealink's existing debt.

The company received a £60 million cash injection from Sweden and immediately launched its Operation Benchmark which looked for restructuring and economies. It was therefore decided during September to shed 1,000 staff at all levels and to close the Folkestone–Boulogne service at the end of the year.

Harwich: With the Stena takeover of Sealink U.K. Ltd., the Harwich–Hook service was transferred to the ownership of Stena Line B.V., the Dutch operating company based in the Hook of Holland. On 31st January all British management ceased.

On 19th June the former *St. Nicholas* (since her January refit renamed *Stena Normandy*) completed her service before sailing to Southampton to take up a new link to Cherbourg.

Taking her place came the former *Silja Regina* which was renamed *Stena Britannica*. She had been built in 1981 for the Stockholm–Helsinki route.

Dover: As part of Stena Line's reorganisation of ships and services, it was decided that the *St. Christopher* would be transferred to Stranraer while the *Stena Cambria* (ex *St. Anselm*) would switch to Holyhead allowing the *Horsa* to return to Folkestone. The 'Christopher' arrived back at Dover from overhaul renamed *Stena Antrim* on 8th February. At the conclusion of her afternoon sailing from Calais on 4th April,

*The **Stena Cambria** arriving at Fishguard. (Miles Cowsill)*

the *Stena Antrim* (ex. *St. Christopher*) destored before sailing to commence her new career in the North Channel.

The Dover–Calais service was set to receive the former D.S.B. (Danish State Railways) ferry *Peder Paars* from the Aarhus-Kalundborg link and for which Stena Line had paid £40 million. Built in 1985 at Nakskov in Denmark, and renamed *Stena Invicta*, the 19,763 gross ton vessel would be accompanied by the £35 million freighter *Stena Challenger*, one of four similar vessels then building in Fosen (Norway). This was necessary as although the 'Invicta's' passenger accommodation was for as many as 1,850, the ship was only built with a single freight deck. The ship commenced service on 27th June under the command of Captain Ron Little.

A further £5 million was spent on refurbishing the *Stena Invicta* before she took up station, under the command of Captain Roger Bell, on 7th July.

The *Stena Fantasia* sailed to Gothenburg in November to receive a replacement bow thrust unit to equal that installed during her conversion at Bremerhaven in addition to a new stern KaMeWa azimuthing thruster. She arrived back in early December with new and smaller funnel markings replacing the original, oversized, Sea Containers version.

Folkestone: With the closure of the 148 year Folkestone–Boulogne route scheduled for 31st December, the *Stena Hengist* completed her service with the 17.00 to Boulogne on Christmas Eve. She sailed for a Birkenhead refit at midday on 28th December. Sistership *Stena Horsa* (Captain Don MacIntosh) duly closed the link with her 13.30 Boulogne sailing and return on the last day of the year before departing from Dover for lay-up at Milford Haven on 4th January 1992.

It had originally been planned for the 'Hengist' to finish service first and for the 'Horsa' to close the service but this was later reversed. However after representations from Ferry Publications (who had just published a book stating that the 'Horsa' would close the route), the company reverted to the original plan. On that final day, Ferry Publications also sold tickets to the Agoudimos family who were anxious to see the ship they wished to acquire. The writers were the last to drive both on and off at Folkestone.

Newhaven: During the early autumn the French management announced that the Newhaven-Dieppe service would be given a further six months in which to resolve the industrial problems which were now making it the most unreliable of all N.W. European ferry services.

*The **Stena Horsa** leaving Folkestone on the final sailing to Boulogne - 31st December 1991. (FotoFlite)*

Southampton: The *Stena Normandy* undertook berthing trials on 20th January prior to her returning to Harwich until June. She opened the new Southampton–Cherbourg service at 23.59 on 28th June. During the peak season the vessel operated from Southampton on a Tuesday, Friday and Sunday at 10.30 and 23.59, with an inward service from Cherbourg at 18.30. On a Monday, Thursday and Saturday, scheduled departure times from Southampton were 16.00 with sailings from Cherbourg at 09.30 and 23.59. On Wednesdays the *Stena Normandy* offered only an 18.30 service from France and a 23.59 sailing from Southampton. From 23rd September, only one round sailing a day was offered. This complicated timetable was later modified to offer more simplistic timings.

Holyhead: Following the announcement that the *St. Columba* would undergo a major £7 million refit, the contract was secured by a German yard. The eight week refit saw all the existing facilities being replaced. A new a la carte restaurant, free-flow restaurant, children's playroom and nursery area, lorry drivers' restaurant, two new shops, Pullman lounge and businessmen's club, show bar, pizza parlour, gambling arcade and Irish bar were installed during this overhaul. The new show bar would provide a new travel concept created by Stena Line in Sweden, giving live entertainment on most sailings with rock bands, country & western and jazz music being offered. The refitted vessel would be the first in the Sealink fleet to convey the much-vaunted Stena Line 'travel service concept,' which was designed to give people the chance of not just travelling from A to B, but the sheer pleasure of being onboard a ship.

Meanwhile, following the departure of the *St. Columba* for her major refit, the *Stena Cambria* replaced her on the route. On 11th February, she holed herself in the inner harbour at Holyhead and as a result had to be sent to Birkenhead for repairs. The *Stena Horsa* was sent from Folkestone to cover her absence taking up the service the next day until the *Earl William* was able to enter service two days later from her lay

The **Stena Normandy** *leaving Southampton for Cherbourg. (Miles Cowsill)*

THE FRENCH CONNECTION

Above: *The Sealink-owned, French-flagged train ferry* **Saint Eloi** *leaving Dover for Dunkerque West. (John Hendy)*

Top Right: *During the 1988 summer season, the* **Saint Eloi** *was chartered to pool-partners S.N.C.F. for the Calais Maritime - Dover Admiralty Pier train connected services. (Miles Cowsill)*

Right: *The vessel was renamed* **Channel Entente** *in May 1989 and was eventually sold to the Isle of Man Steam Packet Company in February 1990. This view shows her non-standard dark blue hull markings. (FotoFlite)*

Above: Stena's reallocation and renaming of ships saw the **Galloway Princess** become the **Stena Galloway** while the **St. David** was renamed **Stena Caledonia**. They are seen together at Stranraer. (Miles Cowsill)

Below: Bathed in golden sunshine, the **Stena Fantasia** is seen arriving off the South Foreland in December 1995 and illustrates the exterior modifications to her paintwork made following Sealink's purchase by Stena Line. (John Hendy)

Right: When in 1992, Stena Line took-over the operation of the Newhaven - Dieppe service, the French vessel **Versailles** was taken on charter and renamed **Stena Londoner**. She is today SeaFrance's **SeaFrance Monet**. (Miles Cowsill)

up on the River Fal. The *Earl William,* with a limited passenger certificate for only 300, was later joined by the *Cambridge Ferry.* On 19th February the 'Cambria' returned to the link on completion of her repairs, which allowed the *Cambridge Ferry* to sail back to Stranraer and the 'William' to lay up once again.

On Thursday, 14th March the *Stena Hibernia* (Captain John Sinnott) re-entered service following her extensive refit.

On 29th June, the *Earl William* re-entered service on the Holyhead–Dun Laoghaire route with the *Stena Hibernia* as the *Stena Cambria* was retained at Dover until the arrival of the *Stena Invicta.* She took up service on the 12.45 sailing from Dun Laoghaire to Holyhead operating with a reduced passenger certificate until the arrival of the 'Cambria'. The 'Cambria' arrived back on 8th July, and took up service some three days later on the 04.00 sailing to Ireland. The *Earl William* then stood down. Meanwhile, the *St. Cybi* (ex. *Stena Sailer*) remained on the link in a supportive role until the end of the summer.

Stranraer: The planned charter of the *Chartres* to cover for the refits of the vessels at Stranraer did not materialise as the former train ferry was required by the French Government for Gulf War operations. The majority of the freight during the overhaul period was conveyed by the *Cambridge Ferry* and the *St. Cybi.* The *Stena Antrim* duly entered service on the link on the 09.30 sailing from Larne on Sunday 7th April. Meanwhile the *Darnia,* which had been on the link for fourteen years, completed her last sailing on 21st February from Larne on the 21.00 sailing to Scotland under the command of Captain Martin Miller. The ship then sailed to Bremerhaven the next day, was handed to her new Swedish owners Nordstrom & Thulin on 5th April and renamed *Nord Neptunus.*

◆ 1992

At the World Travel Fair in London on 16th November, Sealink Stena Line officially changed its name to Stena

The **Stena Invicta** *joined the Calais service in 1991. (John Hendy)*

The **Stena Challenger** entered service in 1991 to provide freight back-up for the **Stena Invicta**. *(John Hendy)*

Sealink Line, "to reflect its Scandinavian ownership and quality service standards." It was now only a matter of time before the Swedes dropped the name 'Sealink' altogether.

It was estimated that Operation Benchmark saved the company some £45 million during the year and one of its directors stated that it was now, "out of intensive care but still convalescing."

Harwich: The freighter *Stena Traveller* (the sister to Dover's *Stena Challenger*) arrived at the Hook from her Norwegian builders on 28th February and after a N.A.T.O. charter took up the Harwich link on 1st April during the 'Seatrader's' refit.

Dover: Although Operation Benchmark had originally planned for the *Stena Challenger* to move from the port, leaving the Sealink fleet with two ships, it was decided to transfer her to freight operations on the Dover–Dunkerque West link to run in conjunction with the S.N.A.T. train ferry *Nord Pas-de-Calais*.

Newhaven: With continued losses and long spates of industrial disputes, Sealink S.N.A.T. duly made a formal announcement on 26th March that they planned to close their historic Dieppe–Newhaven service. In anticipation of this announcement, crews on both ships had gone on strike four days earlier. The *Versailles* was sent to Le Havre, meanwhile the *Champs Elysees* blocked the linkspan at Dieppe, holding not only the company to ransom but the town itself which relied so heavily on the daily traffic from England. S.N.A.T. announced that a number of companies were showing interest in taking over the service from them, including Sealink Stena Line, Corsica Ferries, Sally and B&I Line. Eventually, terms were agreed between the French company and Sealink Stena Line to charter the *Versailles* and *Champs Elysees*. The *Versailles* was sent to Southampton and repainted in the company's livery, given a British crew and renamed *Stena Londoner*. On 22nd May, she left Newhaven and arrived in Dieppe to a welcome by thousands of townspeople lining the quays. As the *Champs Elysees* still blocked the linkspan, she was forced to use the freight berth

*The **Stena Challenger** is seen arriving at Calais in December 1994. (John Hendy)*

The **Stena Antrim** (ex. **St. Christopher**) arriving at Larne during August 1995. (Miles Cowsill)

The **Stena Felicity** *leaving Fishguard. (Miles Cowsill)*

The **Cambridge Ferry** *pictured at Fishguard. (Miles Cowsill)*

in the inner harbour. The striking French crew on board the *Champs Elysees* realised their cause was lost and walked off the vessel some four days later, allowing her then to sail to Southampton to be repainted and renamed *Stena Parisien*. The vessel retained her Dieppe registry and was crewed with French seamen on a non-strike agreement. She subsequently entered service on 3rd June. Confidence to the link under British management was quickly restored and with some aggressive marketing and reduction of fares, the route began to return to profit.

Southampton: The freighter *Stena Traveller* (sister to the *Stena Challenger*) operated to Cherbourg during the summer months allowing the *Stena Normandy* to concentrate on accompanied car traffic.

Fishguard: The *Stena Felicity* went for overhaul during November, her place being taken by the *Stena Cambria* from Holyhead. While she was at the Pembrokeshire port, the French registered *Chartres* covered for her on a short-term charter.

Holyhead: The continued freight boom at Holyhead saw Sealink having to charter the freight vessel *Auersbeg* to support the two passenger ferries on the link for the summer period.

On 28th July the *Stena Cambria* commenced using the new deep water berth at Holyhead because of the tidal restrictions in the inner harbour. The same day the vessel experienced major engine problems and had to be withdrawn from service and the *Stena Galloway* from Stranraer was sent to replace her. After minor repairs to the `Cambria', she was then sent to Stranraer in place of the `Galloway' until mid-August when she returned to Birkenhead for major repairs before returning to her home port on 21st August.

Stranraer: A new fast ferry service between Stranraer and Belfast commenced on 1st June which went into direct competition to Sealink's operations and that of P&O European Ferries at Cairnryan. The service was to prove very successful and was to see a general reduction in fares by both the rival companies. Meanwhile, Sea Containers, who had started the new SeaCat Scotland operation, expressed interest in starting another rival service on the Irish Sea between Holyhead and Dun Laoghaire. Following Sealink refusing slots at both ports, the matter then went to the E.E.C. Commissioners and Sealink were forced to offer operational slots at Holyhead for the company but in the event the rival service failed to materialise.

On 17th December, a crane plunged into the sea at Stranraer, which put the linkspan out of action and for a short period the company were forced to use the P&O European Ferries' terminal at nearby Cairnryan.

Disposals: Following the closure of the Folkestone–Boulogne service, the *Stena Horsa* arrived at Milford Haven on 5th January 1992 to lay up with the *Earl William* and *St. Cybi*, which had completed her last spell in service just before Christmas on the Holyhead-Dun Laoghaire route. The 'Horsa' was subsequently sold to Agoudimos Lines for which she was renamed *Penelope A*. The *Earl William* was also sold to Greek interests later in the summer

and renamed *Pearl William*. Meanwhile, the veteran train ferry *Cambridge Ferry* completed her last sailing on 16th March on the Stranraer–Larne service, the next day she sailed to Milford Haven, via Fishguard, for lay up. A month later, on 21st April, she sailed as the *Ita Uno* prior to taking up service between Bari (Italy) and Durres in Albania. She has since been renamed *Sirio*.

The *Stena Hengist* was not withdrawn from service immediately as she was required on the Irish Sea to cover for the winter refits. The former Folkestone vessel commenced operations on the Irish Sea on 9th January on the Holyhead–Dun Laoghaire route, covering in turn for the refits of the *Stena Cambria* and *Stena Hibernia*. Following completing her stint at the Anglesey port, she sailed north to Stranraer to cover for their overhauls. She completed her final sailing with the company on the 05.30 sailing between Stranraer and Larne on 14th March. Three days later at

From left to right, the **St Cybi**, **Cambridge Ferry** *and* **Earl William** *at Milford Haven. (Miles Cowsill)*

Above: *The **Stena Invicta** (ex. **Peder Paars**) arriving at Calais in March 1994. (John Hendy)*
Top right: *Outward bound from Dun Laoghaire, the fast craft **Stena Sea Lynx II** gathers speed for Holyhead. (Miles Cowsill)*
Below: *The **Stena Hibernia** (ex. **St. Columba**) alongside Holyhead's Salt Island berth in July 1995. (Miles Cowsill)*

Holyhead her funnel was painted white and she was subsequently renamed *Romilda*, following her sale to G.A. Ferries. She trades today for Ventouris Sea Lines as the *Apollo Express 2* operating with her Sealink sister *Senlac* which is now the *Apollo Express I*.

◆ 1993

Dover: The *Chartres* became Sealink's fifth ship on the Dover–Calais link at the end of May but completed service leaving Dover Western Docks at 16.00 on Friday 24th September–the final passenger ship working from the Admiralty Pier. The following day she was chartered by the French Post Office to see the start of the Whitbread Round the World Yacht Race in Spithead before returning to Calais to lay-up. She was sold to Agapitos in December and was renamed *Express Santorini* leaving her home port for Piraeus on 21st December.

Newhaven: Such was the volume of freight on offer on the Newhaven–Dieppe service during the summer that the Italian freight vessel *Vinzia E* (ex. *Wesertal*) was taken on a three month charter starting on 4th June. Meanwhile, work on a new ferry terminal at Dieppe had commenced earlier in the year to allow the ships to berth away from the main town.

Holyhead: In late May, Stena Sealink announced that they planned to open a new fast ferry service between Holyhead and Dun Laoghaire with the new 240 ft. wavepiercer catamaran *Stena Sea Lynx*. The new service would take passengers 1 hour 50 minutes to make the crossing between Wales and Ireland, instead of the conventional ferry timing of 3 hours 30 minutes. Initially it would operate four round sailings a day, which would be reduced for the winter period to three. The new craft would have capacity for 450 passengers and up to 90 cars. On 15th July, Mrs. Glenys Kinnock, wife of Neil Kinnock M.P., dedicated the new service. Some four weeks after the new

*The **Stena Parisien** pictured at the new passenger terminal at Dieppe. (Ferry Publications Library)*

fast craft entered service, she had carried some 58,328 passengers, 12,340 cars and 210 motorbikes, with 100% reliability record. Following the success of the fast ferry service, the company announced that a larger mark II craft would enter service the following summer with an increased capacity for 600 passengers and 140 cars.

Further important high-speed news was announced by Stena Sealink Line on 6th July at a press conference in London. The company announced that they had placed an order for two massive high-speed ferries from Finnyards, Rauma, Finland for delivery in 1995. One of the revolutionary craft would be placed on the Holyhead-Dun Laoghaire service within two years. At the press conference Stena Line A.B., who had ordered the new vessels, claimed they would be a technological breakthrough with both cars and freight being able to be carried on the 40 knot craft. The new HSS (high speed sea service) would boast a length of some 124 metres and a beam of 40 metres and would be able to carry 1,500

passengers and 375 cars or 50 trucks and 100 cars. The craft would be powered by water jets via four gas turbines, which would be able to operate in most weather conditions. Loading and unloading would be via a special stern ramp and anticipated turnrounds would be some 30 minutes at each port. Over the next three years the first craft was developed in great secrecy and eventually made her debut to the press on 20th February 1996, when she arrived off Dover for the first time. The vessel *Stena Explorer* did not enter service until 10th April 1996.

◆ 1994

Dover: The *Stena Challenger* was withdrawn from the Dunkerque West route on 14th March when she was transferred to the Calais link thereby allowing Sealink to operate a five ship service in opposition to P&O European

*Leaving Calais for Dover during March 1994 are the **Stena Challenger** followed by the **Stena Cambria** (ex. **St. Anselm**). (John Hendy)*

Ferries. The ship began operating in a passenger mode as from 24th March duplicating the sailings of the *Stena Cambria* which had been brought back from Holyhead to cover spring overhauls.

Newhaven: The new ferry terminal at Dieppe opened on 22nd July. The *Stena Parisien* made the first commercial sailing there on the 07.30 sailing from Newhaven but it was not until six days later that the company surrendered the old town berth in favour of the new terminal. Three months later, the company announced that the *Stena Sea Lynx II* would be transferred to the Newhaven-Dieppe service in time for the next summer season to introduce a fast ferry service to Dieppe from Sussex in 1 hour 45 minutes. In the event the plan did not materialise and it was not until 1996 that a fast ferry service was established.

Holyhead: Work started during the year in anticipation of the arrival of the new HSS. Similar work commenced at St. Michael's Pier at Dun Laoghaire to accommodate the new operation.

The company's rivals at Holyhead, B&I Line and their now parent company Irish Ferries, announced that they would build a new vessel for their route to Dublin, which would triple their freight capacity and provide an 81% increase in car capacity on the Central Corridor service. The new four engined vessel built in Holland would have an operating speed of 21.5 knots with a car capacity for 600 and a passenger accommodation for 1,700 passengers. With the forthcoming introduction of the HSS, B&I Line had no alternative but to order new tonnage.

The *Stena Sea Lynx II* arrived at Holyhead from Tasmania on the morning of 18th June and was officially named two days later by the wife of the Anglesey M.P. The fast craft entered service on 22nd June on the 07.00 sailing from Holyhead which allowed the renamed, *Stena Sea Lynx I* to sail south to take up service between Fishguard and Rosslare. Meanwhile at Holyhead, the company were to see a 12% increase in passenger figures.

Fishguard: The arrival of the newer and larger *Stena Sea Lynx II* allowed the *Stena Sea Lynx I* to start a new fast ferry service between Fishguard and Rosslare, commencing on 28th June. Initially she operated four round sailings a day and then subsequently these were increased to five a day during the peak period. Like the Holyhead service, the Fishguard route was to attract good loadings and new business. Passenger carryings increased by some 8% by the end of August.

New port facilities at Fishguard were opened for passengers and cars with a new duty-free supermarket, customs hall and marshalling areas.

Stena Sealink Line chartered the *Norrona* for the winter refits on the Irish Sea. Following a short spell initially first at Fishguard, she sailed to Holyhead and then to Stranraer.

The **Stena Sea Lynx** arriving at Rosslare. (Miles Cowsill)

◆ 1995

At a London Press Conference on 12th July, it was announced that the operational partnership between Stena Sealink Line and French partners S.N.A.T. would terminate as from 31st December. Stena Sealink stated that it would, "bring its full weight to bear in the key Continental tourist and freight 'short sea' sector to create an international service organisation capable of challenging any other operator."

Sealink S.N.A.T. would in future trade as SeaFrance and its ships were renamed: *Fiesta–SeaFrance Cezanne, Cote d'Azur–SeaFrance Renoir, Nord Pas-de-Calais–SeaFrance Nord Pas-de-Calais* (until 3rd July 1996), and from 3rd July 1996, *Stena Londoner–SeaFrance Monet*.

Dover: The *Stena Challenger* was blown ashore in a N.E. gale when approaching Calais on 19th September. Some 172 passengers and 73 crew were on board and it was not until the evening of the following day that she was pulled free. Port control at Calais was blamed for the accident as they were not aware of the exact position of the ship which had commenced its approach prior to being informed of another vessel leaving port.

The **Chartres** spent her final seasons at Calais on charter to A.L.A. for the twice daily train connected Western Docks services. (John Hendy)

The **Stena Caledonia** *leaving Larne for Scotland. (Miles Cowsill)*

The ship was eventually moved to Dunkerque for inspection before sailing to A&P Tyne for repairs to her bent hull plates. She re-entered service on the evening of 24th October–the first in the new Stena Line livery which the company had decided to adopt for all its ships.

The Dover–Dunkerque train ferry service finally ended on 22nd December after which the *Nord Pas-de-Calais* was sent for overhaul before re-entering service on the Calais link on 7th January 1996.

Newhaven: The *Stena Sea Lynx II* made a press debut at Dieppe and Newhaven on 6th and 7th February, in anticipation of her transfer to the route. In the event, following this high profile trip, the new service was postponed until 1996. Meanwhile, following the demise of her charter on the Folkestone–Boulogne route (where she had served as Meridian Ferries' *Spirit of Boulogne*), the *Marine Evangeline* was chartered in late June to support the passenger services.

The *Stena Londoner* completed her final sailing on the Dieppe service on 2nd March 1996 before sailing to cover for overhauls at Fishguard and Holyhead. On 18th April she completed her last sailing at Holyhead and then sailed to Newhaven for destoring and was disposed of on 6th May Today she operates from Calais to Dover as SeaFrance's *SeaFrance Monet*. The new fast ferry service started in the light of an 18.4% drop in passenger traffic during 1995. The former strike-ridden service had seen a steady growth for the last two years but with the increased competition and opening of the Channel Tunnel, passenger figures had dropped.

Southampton: Meanwhile, at Southampton at the turn of the year, it seemed likely that the *Stena Normandy* would spend her last season on the Southampton-Cherbourg service and possibly would be replaced by a fast craft from Portsmouth during 1997.

The **Stena Challenger** *on the beach at Calais. (Ferry Publications Library)*

The **Stena Londoner** *arriving at Dieppe. (Miles Cowsill)*

Fishguard: During March, Stena Line announced that they planned to build a new ferry for their Gothenburg–Frederikshavn service and that the *Stena Jutlandica* would be transferred to the U.K. At the time of the announcement, it was envisaged that she would replace the *Stena Felicity* on the Fishguard service when her charter ended during March 1996. In the event, nothing came of these anticipated plans for Fishguard and the former Swedish ship was earmarked for the Dover–Calais route to challenge the Channel Tunnel.

Meanwhile, the *Norrona* was chartered again by the company to allow the *Stena Antrim* to cover on the Irish Sea at Holyhead and Fishguard.

Just before the demise of trading name Sealink, the company secured a further year's charter of the *Stena Felicity* at Fishguard until April 1997.

Holyhead: A new Holyhead-Dublin freight ferry service started as from 2nd November using the *Stena Traveller*. The introduction of this new dedicated freight operation was in response to Irish Ferries' success with their new passenger/freight vessel *Isle of Innisfree*. Two round sailings a day would be operated by the *Stena Traveller*, a sister of the *Stena Challenger* at Dover. The route initially commenced using the chartered *Marine Evangeline* on 13th October 1995.

The *Stena Hibernia*, which had played an important role at Holyhead for over eighteen years, was repainted and renamed *Stena Adventurer* in anticipation of her transfer to Dover from the Irish Sea on the arrival of the HSS. In the event, the vessel was not put on the Dover Strait but was to remain at Holyhead in a supportive role to the HSS.

Stranraer: Mounting speculation continued throughout 1995 that Sealink would withdraw their operations from

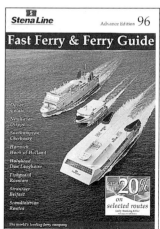

Larne in favour of Belfast. The company also decided to introduce their second new HSS on the North Channel which further fuelled the view that they would transfer there.

The move was made on 12th November with the *Stena Antrim* completing the last sailing from Larne the previous day.

At midnight on 31st December 1995, Stena Sealink Line adopted the trading name of Stena Line.

Postscript

◆ **1996**

Dover: The *Stena Cambria* (ex. *St. Anselm*) returned to the route for which she was built on 19th January while high speed operations commenced on 13th February with the *Stena Lynx II* taking up service. The fast craft was called away to Gothenburg on 9th May but on 28th June the larger *Stena Lynx III* arrived at Dover from InCat in Tasmania and took up the link on 4th July.

After an £8 million refit, the former Gothenburg–Frederikshavn ferry *Stena Jutlandica* commenced service as the *Stena Empereur* on 16th August. With a capacity for 2,300 passengers, 500 cars and 85 freight units, the 28,727 gross ton ferry is the largest ever to operate across the Dover Strait. She replaced the *Stena Challenger* when she was transferred to Holyhead.

Stranraer: The *Stena Voyager* (the second HSS) commenced service on 21st July, which allowed the *Stena Antrim* to lay-up at Bellfast. Meanwhile the *Stena Caledonia* and *Stena Galloway* were retained on the route operating both as passenger and freight ships. The *Stena Antrim* had to be brought back into service because the *Stena Voyager* was unable to cope with the rosters due to longer passage times than anticipated.

Above: The HSS that never operated under the Sealink name. (Ferry Publications Library)
*Below: The **Stena Felicity** pictured in the new Stena Line livery. (Miles Cowsill)*

Sealink's Inland and Coastal services

Lake Windermere: The smallest Sealink ships were the four passenger launches that plied the placid waters of Lake Windermere in England's Lake District. All four vessels had an historic railway ancestry, the *Tern* (120 gross tons) of 1891 being the oldest. In addition there were the *Swift* (203 gross tons) of 1900, the *Teal* (251 gross tons) of 1936 and the *Swan* (251 gross tons) of 1938.

Their services commenced at Easter and then ran through the season from May until October linking the former railhead at Lakeside with Bowness and Ambleside.

The economic situation saw the *Swift* laid-up in 1982 but Sealink took over the operation of the Lake Coniston vessel *Gondola* before it passed to the National Trust in 1983.

Following the acquisition of Sealink by Sea Containers, in 1985 the Windermere services were transferred to the ownership of their Hotels & Leisure Division subsidiary, SeaCo Inc. The operation later traded as the Windermere Iron Steamboat Company.

The Humber: Maintaining the ferry link across the Humber for many years were the paddle steamer sisters *Tattershall Castle* and *Wingfield Castle*. They were both built in 1934 by William Grey & Co. at West Hartlepool. Of 556 gross tons, they each carried in the region of 20 cars and about 940 passengers. The *Lincoln Castle* joined the service from New Holland to Hull in 1940. She was built on the Clyde by A.& J. Inglis, was 598 gross tons and boasted similar capacity to that of her running partners.

During the period of the 1972 coal miners' strike, fuel for the three coal fired paddle steamers was almost exhausted and the local passenger excursion vessel *Flamborian* was chartered to keep the service going.

The status quo was finally broken in September 1972 when the *Tattershall Castle* was withdrawn and later sold for static use on the Thames. After a period of lay-up at Immingham, the vessel was placed in position on the Thames Embankment in December 1975. She originally opened as an art gallery but in January 1981 was purchased by Chef & Brewer (Grand Metropolitan Hotels) and remains

The **Swan** *was one of four Sealink vessels employed on Lake Windermere. (John Collins)*

a popular leisure venue and bar up-river from Hungerford Bridge.

The *Wingfield Castle* was finally withdrawn from service on 14th March 1974 and taking her place on the Humber crossing, as from 4th February, came the diesel electric paddle vessel *Farringford* which had been replaced on the Yarmouth (Isle of Wight)–Lymington crossing. In preparation for her new role, her bow and stern ramps were removed and she was converted to side loading. The 'Wingfield' was originally purchased for £30,000 by the Brighton Marina Company although it was stated that another £80,000 would be spent on refurbishment. She was to be renamed *Brighton Belle* and was towed from New Holland to the Alexandra Dock in Hull on 29th May. On 1st July the tug *Sun XXVI* towed the paddler to the Royal Albert Dock in London.

After it was shown that she was too large to enter the Brighton Marina, the *Wingfield Castle* was sold to Shepherdswood Studios and later to Whitbread and after periods of lay-up on the Thames below Tower Bridge and, by 1982, at Rochester, she finally found her way to Swansea where permission for the brewery to use her was unforthcoming. She was finally sold again during autumn 1985 and moved back to her birthplace at Hartlepool where she became a 'living museum piece.' Work was carried out by the craftsmen who had recently restored the ironclad battleship, *Warrior*.

Whilst on passage to New Holland with the 06.30 sailing on 8th January 1977, the *Lincoln Castle* severely damaged a paddle float as a result of which her passengers were landed by pilot boat. The paddler was later towed to New Holland but with the *Farringford* away on overhaul, until the 'Lincoln' returned to service four days later, passengers between Hull and New Holland had to travel by bus–a journey time of 2 hours.

Meanwhile, the *Farringford* was taken out of service on 12th November 1977 for dry docking at Immingham where it was discovered that her entire hull below the water line required replating at a cost of some £140,000.

Worse was to happen when during the *Lincoln Castle's* next refit, on 17th March 1978 it was discovered that she immediately required a new boiler which would take nine months to obtain at a cost of £150,000. With the imminent opening of the new Humber Bridge, the ship was immediately withdrawn from service. After the National Railway Museum had rejected her and plans to use her as a maritime museum had foundered, in 1980 she was sold to Mr. Francis Daly, a local nightclub owner, who eventually berthed her immediately down river from the new bridge. The vessel lies today at the Grimsby Heritage Centre.

For three weeks during January 1979, the spare Lymington ferry *Freshwater* was brought in to cover the *Farringford's* overhaul having herself been fitted with side doors during her autumn 1978 refit at Southampton. Bow damage to the *Farringford* during October saw the charter of the Bridlington pleasure boat *Yorkshire Belle*.

In January 1980, the *Freshwater* came north again after having put into Dover with engine troubles en route.

The *Farringford* was off service twice during February 1980 when the *Yorkshire Belle* was again required.

The Humber Bridge finally opened for traffic on 24th June 1981 with the last train connected services to and from Grimsby being made at 10.30 from Hull and 11.30 from New Holland. A 'Farewell Trip' was later made at 17.30 from Hull and 18.15 from New Holland. So ended the 178 years of the Humber ferry after which the *Farringford* was sent to lay-up in the Alexandra Dock at Hull.

On passage to New Holland is the **Wingfield Castle**. *(Ferry Publications Library)*

The **Farringford** closed the Humber ferry in 1981. Cars were parked on her after end to avoid being covered in spray. *(R.B. Adams)*

During October the Scottish operators Western Ferries purchased the 33 year old vessel for an expanded service on the Clyde. In the event the new service failed to materialise and the vessel was broken up at Silcock's Basin in Hull during March 1984.

Tilbury–Gravesend: The Tilbury–Gravesend ferry was operated by the 213 gross ton sisterships *Catherine* and *Edith*, which were both built at White's yard at Southampton in 1960. The third vessel *Rose*, had been transferred to the the Caledonian Steam Packet Company in 1967 where she became their *Keppel* for the link to Great Cumbrae. Each vessel carried 475 passengers on the Thames service.

With the growth of vehicle traffic through the Dartford Tunnel on the nearby M25 and the decline of dock labour required at nearby Tilbury, the route progressively lost money. British Rail/Sealink attempted to rid themselves of their obligations to operate the link but no other company was interested in its costly operation.

In an effort to save running costs, during 1977 the company repurchased their former Dartmouth–Kingswear ferries *Adrian Gilbert* and *Humphrey Gilbert* for £20,000 from the St. Maws Ferry Co. of Falmouth. Both were re-engined and Class 5 certificates for 100 people were applied for. Much to Sealink's displeasure, the vessels failed to gain the Department of Transport's approval having low freeboard and limited covered accommodation. Both were put up for sale in December and were soon back in operation in the west of England.

The *Catherine* was decommissioned during 1981 and cannibalised for spares to keep the service in operation with the *Edith*. In September 1989, the spare ship was eventually purchased by the Newcastle-based company, Open Leisure who planned to operate the renamed *Catherine Wheel* on cruises on the River Tyne. After a thorough refit, during which time she was given a bogus stern wheel, the cruises commenced in June 1990.

Sea Containers had planned to remove the *Edith* to the Solent where she would be used in a cruising role while finding a more efficient, cost-effective, vessel for the Thames.

The Tilbury–Gravesend service was eventually sold to White Horse Ferries on 4th March 1991 and when on 30th

The **Catherine** arriving at Tilbury. (Jim Ashby Collection)

June 1992 their locally-built, 95 passenger catamaran *Great Expectations* was eventually placed on the link, the last of the original Sealink trio was laid-aside at Tilbury.

At the time of writing, White Horse Ferries were planning to start a new Thames service at Easter 1997 linking Charing Cross Pier with Canary Wharf and it is their intention to convert the *Edith* to become the route's maintenance vessel.

Isle of Wight: Sealink's Isle of Wight services covered two passenger/vehicle ferry routes from Portsmouth to Fishbourne and Lymington to Yarmouth in addition to the rail connected passenger-only link between Portsmouth Harbour and Ryde Pierhead. As these services were excluded from the sale of Sealink U.K. Ltd. to Stena Line, they are only dealt with until 1990.

Sea Containers retained ownership of the service until five years later, Wightlink was sold to CIN Ven Ltd. (one of Europe's largest venture capital companies) for a reported £107 million.

No new ships were added to the fleet during this period.

Portsmouth–Fishbourne: During 1970 the route was maintained by the 1961 double-ended sisters *Fishbourne*

and *Camber Queen* (built by Philip of Dartmouth with capacity for 168 passengers and 34 cars) in addition to the first of the new ferries, the 1969-built *Cuthred*. This vessel had been constructed for £275.000 at Richards yard at Lowestoft and had entered service the previous June boasting capacity for 745 passengers and 48 cars.

With mainly holiday-based traffic on offer, the route was very much of a seasonal nature but with commercial vehicle traffic on the increase, the *Cuthred's* entry into service was not before time.

A fourth ship was launched from the Robb Caledon yard at Dundee on 3rd May 1973 in the form of the *Caedmon* - the first of a trio of sisterships (the other two for Lymington) which were in every way improved versions of the *Cuthred*. The £1.8 million *Caedmon's* capacity was for 750 passengers and 52 cars and she entered service on 27th July.

With the gradual increase in traffic, severe capacity problems were encountered at the Broad Street terminal at Portsmouth but the closure of the city's old power station at the Gunwharf provided the answer. A £2 million loan was arranged for its purchase and the new terminal was duly opened on 21st February 1982. The old slipway method of loading was replaced by the use of a linkspan and in June

1983, similar facilities were opened at Fishbourne.

The first of a new generation of Isle of Wight vehicle ferries was launched at Henry Robb's Leith yard on 30th March 1983. This was the £5 million *St. Catherine* which entered service on 3rd July. With passenger capacity for as many as 1,000 passengers and 142 cars, for the first time passengers were asked to vacate their cars during the passage. The *Fishbourne* was duly retired on the *St. Catherine's* entry into service although she was briefly brought back for 48 hours when in early September the *Caedmon* developed engine problems.

A sistership, named *St. Helen* was launched at Robb's Leith yard on 15th September 1982 and entered service on 28th November. In readiness for privatisation neither new ship entered service with the B.R. arrow logo on their red funnels.

Of the smaller ferries, the *Camber Queen* was in the better condition and was duly sold early in 1984 to the Portuguese company Transado Transportes Fluviais do Sado of Setubal for the 15 minute service from Setubal to Troia. She remains in service today as the *Mira Troia*. The *Fishbourne* was also sold early in 1984 to Pound's scrapyard at Tipner near Portsmouth but was later resold to Seagull Marine Ltd. of Kyrenia, Turkish Cyprus. After a refit

The **Farringford** (left) and **Lymington** during their final 1973 season on the western Solent route. (John Hendy)

The car ferry **Cuthred** (left) is about to be passed by the **Brading** in
the approaches at Portsmouth Harbour during 1981. (John Hendy)

The **Camber Queen** on passage to Fishbourne during 1973. (John
Hendy)

at Chatham she left as *Kypros I* in May 1984. Renamed
Kibris I, she sank in the early hours of 4th February 1985
after being swamped at her moorings in a N.N.W. gale.

The arrival of the *St. Helen* also replaced the *Caedmon*
which switched to Lymington to join her twin sisters.
Meanwhile the *Cuthred* was retained for summer work but
the third 'Saint' class vessel *St. Cecilia* was duly launched
on 4th November 1986 and entered service on 27th March
1987 after which the *Cuthred* was retired from the fleet. Due
to the closure of the Robb yard, the new ship was
constructed at the Cochrane yard at Selby.

The *Cuthred* arrived under tow in the Tyne on 23rd
November 1988 after having languished at Lymington for
two years. Her new owners were Open Leisure, who had
also purchased the former Tilbury ferry *Catherine*. Nothing
came of the plans to convert the former Isle of Wight ferry
into a Mississippi-style cruiser and she was sold on to the
same Portuguese company who had previously purchased
the *Camber Queen*.

On her way back south, on 12th February 1990 she put
into Newhaven to shelter from bad weather before
continuing her voyage to Portugal. The *Cuthred* is presently
the *Mira Praia*.

The fourth 'Saint' also came from the Selby yard and

was launched as the *St. Faith* on 28th March 1990, entering
service on 16th July. Although by this time Sealink had
been taken-over by Stena Line, the Isle of Wight services
were not included in the sale. Thus for her first season in
service, the *St. Faith* carried the livery of a company to
whom she did not belong.

On 7th November 1990, Sea Containers unveiled the
new brand name and livery of Wightlink.

Lymington–Yarmouth: During 1970 the western
Solent link to the Isle of Wight was operated by the three
car ferries: *Lymington* (built by Denny of Dumbarton in
1938 and capable of accommodating 400 passengers and
16 cars), the diesel electric paddle vessel *Farringford* (built
by Denny in 1948–800 passengers and 32 cars) and the
Freshwater (built by Ailsa at Troon in 1959–620 passengers
and 26 cars).

By 1967, the route carried 109,000 cars and in order for
the frequency of crossings to be increased during 1971,
dredging in the Lymington River allowed two vessels to
pass each other within its narrow confines.

Three identical sisters were ordered from Robb Caledon
at Dundee for delivery in 1973. The first was the *Caedmon*,
destined for the Portsmouth station, meanwhile the second

The **St. Catherine** at Portsmouth. (Jim Ashby collection)

and third were the *Cenwulf* and *Cenred*. The *Cenwulf* was launched on 1st June and entered service on 18th October 1973 replacing the *Lymington* which finished on 9th November.

Although named on 29th June, gales prevented the *Cenred* from being launched until 3rd July. She eventually took up the passage in the following January displacing the *Farringford* which had ended her association with the Yarmouth route the day before the *Lymington*.

The new ships boasted capacity for 750 passengers and 52 cars. The *Freshwater* was retained in a summer back-up and relief role until her withdrawal at the close of the 1983 season. All three ferries in service during 1970 passed into the ownership of Western Ferries (Clyde) Ltd. for their route across the Clyde between Hunter's Quay (Dunoon) and McInroy's Point.

In 1988 the former *Lymington* (then trading as the *Sound of Sanda*) celebrated fifty years in service–an outstanding record. During summer 1989 she was used in a daily freight capacity between Port Glasgow and Faslane after which she was laid aside and various schemes to preserve her failed. The *Sound of Sanda* was eventually resold during March 1994 for use as a workboat and was reduced to a hulk on Loch Etive in July 1995.

The *Farringford* (see Humber section) never operated for her new owners but the *Freshwater* (as the *Sound of Seil*) commenced operations on 18th June 1986 and remained in service until July 1995. She was sold to Widnes shipbreakers S. Evans & Sons in summer 1996 for use as a crane barge.

Sealink had previously sold her to the local Portsmouth scrapyard, H.G. Pounds, who later 'resold' her to a Lebanese businessman for a projected route linking Cyprus and Turkey. There was an uproar over the reported sale as the media believed that the ship would be used by the Christian militia running guns into war-torn Beirut. The 'sale' failed to take place and she was duly purchased by Western Ferries in December 1985.

With the new ferries in service on the Lymington route during 1973, in their first year they shipped 179,000 cars. The entry into service of the *St. Catherine* and the *St. Helen* allowed the *Caedmon* to join her twin sisters during November 1983.

Lack of extra capacity became an increasing problem

The first of the Portsmouth 'Saint' class ships, the **St. Catherine** *approaching Fishbourne in April 1989. (John Hendy)*

and during the winter 1977–78 the fitting of mezzanine decks increased car capacity to 70. The construction of linkspans at Lymington in 1976 and Yarmouth in 1983 enabled speedier turnrounds and easier embarkation.

Plans have been drawn up for replacement ships but the harbour authority at Lymington refuses to allow larger vessels for fear of creating greater wash thereby disturbing yachts in the river and causing bank erosion. The provision of new tonnage is now something of a matter of urgency but any moves to do so would be environmentally very sensitive.

Portsmouth–Ryde: The Portsmouth–Ryde route was the oldest Sealink route to the island, tracing its routes back to the earliest years of steam navigation in the area.

September 1969 had seen the withdrawal of the route's last paddle steamer, the 1937-built *Ryde*, which eventually passed for static use on the River Medina between East Cowes and Newport.

The summer of 1970 saw the three diesel sistership *Southsea* and *Brading* (built in 1948 by Denny of Dumbarton) in service with their slightly modified sister, the 1951-built *Shanklin*. The B.R. subsidiary Seaspeed was operating hovercraft on the link (and also from both

*Catamaran **Our Lady Patricia** on passage to Portsmouth in August 1990. (John Hendy)*

*The **Freshwater** approaching Lymington in August 1979. (John Hendy)*

Southampton and Portsmouth to Cowes) during this period but operations from Portsmouth were terminated on 7th September 1972.

Fast craft were tried again during March 1980 when Sealink chartered the high speed catamaran *Highland Seabird* from Western Ferries for a week of trials.

The three Denny-built passenger vessels carried as many as 1,331 passengers (originally in two classes) and were ideal for operating the high capacity route particularly during summer Saturdays when the mass exodus of holidaymakers commenced. The old order changed when in March 1980 the *Shanklin* was withdrawn from service with mechanical problems. During October she was sold for £25,000 to supporters of the preserved paddle steamer *Waverley* and became their *Prince Ivanhoe*. Sadly during her first season of excursion sailings on the Bristol Channel, on 3rd August 1981 she struck an uncharted object off Port Eynon, West Glamorgan, was holed, beached, flooded and subsequently written-off.

Various plans were announced for high speed craft to replace the *Southsea* and *Brading* during the 1980s. In 1982 it was stated that three Norwegian-built catamarans each carrying 500 passengers across Spithead in 10 minutes would be in service for the 1983 season. But it was decided

that so much money had been spent on the new car ferries *St. Catherine* and *St. Helen* that investment for fast craft would have to await privatisation.

A token high speed presence was forthcoming when during summer 1983, the charter was taken of the Vosper Hovermarine HM 218 SES *Ryde Rapide*. When in July 1984, Sea Containers purchased Sealink the twin ferries could claim to have lasted for the whole of the nationalised era. There were immediate plans to replace them firstly with three Hovermarine hovercraft when it was also announced that the *Southsea* would be converted to an Edwardian-style cruise vessel. Then during November 1984 more plans were announced for new craft with three 351 seater Marinjet catamarans from Sweden. The first was due in service on 1st July 1985 but due to a misunderstanding between Sea Containers and the builders, it was sold beforehand and the order was duly cancelled.

International Catamarans of Hobart, Tasmania, were then contacted to provide a pair of £1.9 million craft capable of carrying 448 passengers across Spithead in 15 minutes. It was planned to keep the *Brading* (the most unreliable of the diesel twins) in service until March 1986 but following a period of mechanical problems she was finally withdrawn from service on 21st February that year. Many of her useful

The **Southsea** and **Brading** pass each other at the entrance to Portsmouth Harbour. (Ferry Publications Library)

mechanical parts were removed to keep her sister in 'spares.' She was sold to Portsmouth shipbreakers, H.G. Pounds and in spite of several schemes to purchase her for both operational and static nightclub use, nothing came of these plans and demolition commenced during August 1994. On 1st November, sparks from a welder's torch set the remains of the ship alight and her twisted mass provided a pre-Firework Night 'spectacular' for the residents of northern Portsmouth.

On 17th March 1986 the first 'cat', *Our Lady Patricia*, arrived at Antwerp as deck cargo, reaching Portsmouth, via Folkestone, the following day. Entry into service was 29th March while the second craft, *Our Lady Pamela* arrived at Portsmouth on 30th July taking up the service on 9th August. The *Southsea* duly stood down and after 38 years was relegated to the role of relief ship.

The *Southsea* was retained for the summers of 1987 and 1988 and operated cruises within the Solent area. At the finish of her 1987 season she sailed back to the Clyde on charter to the Waverley Steam Navigation Company whose paddle steamer had failed in her fortieth year.

Two poor summers, a lack of suitable piers to berth alongside, a degree of disinterest from certain managers plus the problems of operating a large excursion ship in an area already flooded with small excursion vessels contributed towards her downfall and she was withdrawn at the end of her 1988 season (her fortieth) on 15th September. Without the high-capacity *Southsea* to assist during the summer Saturday scramble to and from the island, Sealink chartered two small excursion vessels, *Solent Scene* and *Solent Enterprise* to assist the catamarans.

On 13th June 1989 the *Southsea* sailed from Portsmouth to lay-up in the Fal but on 7th May 1992 she returned to Newhaven under tow where, at the time of writing, she still lies. Plans to use her as a night club in Salford Docks for eight months a year were abandoned during 1992.

This historic vessel remains in the ownership of Sea Containers.

FLEET LIST

The end of an era. The final Sealink passenger steamer, *Caesarea* about to sail from Folkestone to Boulogne on 4th October 1980. (John Hendy)

PASSENGER/VEHICLE/RO-RO FREIGHT VESSELS IN REGULAR SERVICE (EXCLUDING SHORT TERM CHARTERS AND CARGO VESSELS) 1970-1995

Name	Builder	Year	Gross tonnage	Freight/car capacity	Passengers	Sealink route	Other information
HARWICH							
Avalon	A. Stephen & Sons Ltd, Linthouse, UK.	1963	6,584	198	750	Harwich-Hook of Holland Irish Sea	Used also as cruise ship. Converted to a car ferry in 1975 for the Fishguard-Rosslare service. 1981 sold for scrap in Pakistan.
St. George	Swan Hunter Tyneside Shipbuilders, Wallsend, UK.	1968	7,356	220	1,200 day service 560 berths night service	Harwich-Hook of Holland	Sold to Greece in 1984. Renamed **Patra Express**. Resold and named **Scandinavian Sky II**, then **Scandinavian Dawn**.
St. Edmund	Cammell Laird Shipbuilders Ltd, Birkenhead, UK.	1975	8,987	296	1,400 day service. 671 berths night service	Harwich-Hook of Holland	Used during the Falklands War. 1985 Sold to M.O.D. renamed **Keren**, then **Scirocco** (Cenargo), **Rozel** (BCIF), **Scirocco**
St. Nicholas	Arendalsvarvet Shipyard, Gothenburg, Sweden	1981	17,043	480	2,100	Harwich-Hook of Holland Southampton-Cherbourg	ex **Prinsessan Birgitta**. Withdrawn from the Hook of Holland service in June 1991. Renamed **Stena Normandy**.
Suffolk Ferry	John Brown & Co, Clydebank, UK.	1947	3,134	-	12	Harwich-Zeebrugge	Train ferry. Withdrawn from service 1980. Scrapped Belgium.
Norfolk Ferry	John Brown & Co, Clydebank, UK.	1951	3,157	-	12	Harwich-Zeebrugge Harwich-Dunkerque	Train ferry. Withdrawn from service 1980. Scrapped Holland in 1983.
Essex Ferry	John Brown & Co, Clydebank, UK.	1957	3,242	-	12	Harwich-Zeebrugge Harwich-Dunkerque	Train ferry. Withdrawn from service 1982. Scrapped Kent in 1983, hulk towed to Norway.
Cambridge Ferry	Hawthorn Leslie (Shipbuilders) Ltd, Hebburn, UK.	1963	3,294	-	12	Harwich-Zeebrugge Harwich-Dunkerque	Train ferry. After the closure of the train ferry service from Harwich & Dover used on Irish Sea freight services. Sold in 1992 renamed **Ita Uno**, then **Sirio**.
Speedlink Vanguard	A.Vuyk & Zonen's Scheepswerven BV, Germany	1973	2,638	-	12	Harwich-Zeebrugge Harwich-Dunkerque	Built as **Stena Shipper**. Converted to train ferry. Withdrawn in 1988 and returned to Stena Line., chartered and then sold to Brittany Ferries, renamed **Normandie Shipper.**
TILBURY							
Catherine	White & Co Ltd. Southampton, UK.	1961	213	-	475	Tilbury-Gravesend	Sold 1989 for cruising on the River Tyne. Renamed **Catherine Wheel** then **Catherine**.
Edith	White & Co Ltd. Southampton, UK.	1961	213	-	475	Tilbury-Gravesend	Laid-up in 1992.
DOVER							
Shepperton Ferry	Swan Hunter & Wigham Richardson Ltd, Wallsend, UK.	1935	2,996	25	500	Dover-Dunkerque	Train ferry. Withdrawn from service in 1972. Sold for scrap in Spain.
Twickenham Ferry	Swan Hunter & Wigham Richardson Ltd, Wallsend, UK.	1936	2,996	25	500	Dunkerque-Dover	Train ferry. Under the management of A.L.A. Withdrawn from service in 1973. Sold for scrap in Spain.
Saint Eloi / Channel Entente	Cantieri Navali di Pietra Ligure, Italy	1974	4,469	160	1,000	Dunkerque-Dover Calais-Dover	Train ferry. Under ownership of ALA. 1989: renamed **Channel Entente**. 1990: Sold to I.O.M.S.P. Co. Ltd and renamed **King Orry**.
Invicta	Wm. Denny & Bros. Ltd, Dumbarton, UK.	1940	4,191	-	1,400	Dover-Calais	Withdrawn from service 1972. Sold for scrap in Holland.
Maid of Orleans	Wm. Denny & Bros. Ltd, Dumbarton, UK.	1949	3,777	30 winter only	1,400	Dover-Folkestone-Calais/Boulogne	Withdrawn from service 1975. Sold for scrap in Spain.

PASSENGER/VEHICLE/RO-RO FREIGHT VESSELS IN REGULAR SERVICE (EXCLUDING SHORT TERM CHARTERS AND CARGO VESSELS) 1970-1995

Name	Builder	Year	Gross tonnage	Freight/car capacity	Passengers	Sealink route	Other information
Lord Warden	Wm. Denny & Bros. Ltd, Dumbarton, UK.	1952	3,333	120	700	Dover-Boulogne Irish Sea	Withdrawn from service 1979. Sold Saudi Arabia renamed **Al Zaher**. Broken up in Pakistan 1981.
Maid of Kent	Wm. Denny & Bros. Ltd, Dumbarton, UK.	1959	3,920	190	1,000	Dover-Boulogne Weymouth-Cherbourg	Withdrawn from service 1981. Sold for scrap in Spain.
Normannia	Wm. Denny & Bros. Ltd, Dumbarton, UK.	1952	2,217	111	500	Dover-Boulogne as from 1964 Weymouth-Channel Islands	Converted to car ferry in 1964. Withdrawn from service 1978. Sold for scrap in Spain.
St. Patrick	Cammell Laird & Co. Ltd, Birkenhead, UK.	1948	3,482		1,200	Folkestone/Dover-Calais/Boulogne	Withdrawn from service 1971. Sold Greece and renamed **Thermopylae**, then **Agapitos I**. Broken up Greece 1979.
Earl Leofric	Hawthorn Leslie (Shipbuilders) Ltd, Hebburn-on-Tyne, UK.	1965	3,879	205	725*	Dover-Boulogne/Calais Irish Sea	ex **Holyhead Ferry I**. Converted to drive-through 1976. Withdrawn from service 1980. Sold for scrap in Spain.
Earl Siward	Swan Hunter Shipbuilders Ltd, UK.	1965	3,602	205	725*	Dover-Boulogne/Calais Irish Sea	ex **Dover**. Converted to drive-through 1977. Withdrawn from service 1981. Sold Cypres and renamed **Sol Express**. 1986 Tyne nightclub **Tuxedo Royale**.
Seafreight Freeway	Appriania Marina di Carpara, Italy.	1981	5,088	1350 lane metres	92	Dover-Zeebrugge Dover-Dunkerque	Built as the **Lucky Rider**. 1985 purchased by Stena line, renamed **Stena Driver**. Sold to Sealink in 1985. Sold to Bulgarian Government in 1988 and renamed **Serdica**, then sold to DSB renamed **Ask**.
Seafreght Highway	Appriania Marina di Carpara, Italy.	1981	5,088	1350 lane metres	92	Dover-Zeebrugge Dover-Dunkerque Holyhead-Dun Laoghaire	Built as the **Easy Rider**. Sold to Sealink in 1985. Sold to Bulgarian Government in 1988 renamed **Boyana**, then sold to DSB renamed **Urd**.
Stena Fantasia	Kockums Varv (Shipyard) AB, Malmo, Sweden	1979	25,243	723	1,800	Dover-Calais	ex **Scandinavia**, ex **Tzarevetz**, ex **Fiesta**.
Stena Invicta	Nakskov, Denmark	1985	19,763	330	2,400	Dover-Calais	ex. **Peder Paars**. Sold to Sealink 1990.
Stena Challenger	Fosen Mek Verkteder, Norway	1990	18,523	84 Lorries	150	Dover-Calais Dover-Dunkerque	On charter from Stena Line Rederi, AB

FOLKESTONE

Name	Builder	Year	Gross tonnage	Freight/car capacity	Passengers	Sealink route	Other information
Stena Horsa	Arsenal de la Marine National Francaise, Brest, France.	1972	5,590	210	1,400	Folkestone-Boulogne Holyhead-Dun Laoghaire	Withdrawn from service 1991. Sold to Greece and renamed **Penelope A**.
Stena Hengist	Arsenal de la Marine National Francaise, Brest, France.	1972	5,590	210	1,400	Folkestone-Boulogne	Withdrawn from service 1991. Sold to Greece and renamed **Romilda**, then **Apollo Express 2**.
Vortigern	Swan Hunter Shipbuilders, Wallsend, UK.	1969	4,371	280	1,000	Folkestone/Dover-Calais/Boulogne/Dunkerque	Withdrawn from service 1988. Sold to Greece and renamed **Milos Express**.

NEWHAVEN

Name	Builder	Year	Gross tonnage	Freight/car capacity	Passengers	Sealink route	Other information
Falaise	Wm. Denny & Bros. Ltd, UK.	1947	2,416	96	700	Newhaven-Dieppe Weymouth-Channel Islands	Withdrawn from service 1974. Converted to car ferry in 1964. Sold for scrap in Spain.
Senlac	Arsenal de la Marine National Francaise, Brest, France.	1972	5.590	210	1,400	Newhaven-Dieppe	Withdrawn from service 1987. Sold to Greece and renamed **Apollo Express I**.
Stena Londoner	Joza Lozovina Mosor, Yugoslavia.	1973	6,737	425	1,800	Dieppe-Newhaven	ex **Stena Nordica**, ex **Stena Danica**, ex **Stena Nautica**, ex **Versailles**. To SeaFrance in 1996 renamed **SeaFrance Monet** (Calais-Dover).

Name	Builder	Year	Gross tonnage	Freight/car capacity	Passengers	Sealink route	Other information
Stena Parisien	Dubigenon Normandie, Nantes, France.	1984	9,069	330	1,800	Calais-Dover Dieppe-Newhaven	ex **Champs Elysees.** SNCF: Calais-Dover transferred to Dieppe service in 1990. Renamed 1992.
ISLE OF WIGHT							
Brading	Wm. Denny & Bros. Ltd, Dumbarton, UK.	1948	837	-	1,331	Portsmouth-Ryde	Withdrawn from service 1986. Scrapped 1995.
Southsea	Wm. Denny & Bros. Ltd, Dumbarton, UK.	1948	837	-	1,331	Portsmouth-Ryde	Withdrawn from service 1988. Laid up at Newhaven under the ownership of Sea Containers.
Shanklin	Wm. Denny & Bros. Ltd, Dumbarton, UK.	1951	833	-	1,331	Portsmouth-Ryde	Withdrawn from service 1980. Sold to Waverley Excursions renamed **Prince Ivanhoe**. Lost August 1981.
Our Lady Pamela	International Catamarans, Hobart, Australia.	1986	312		470	Portsmouth-Ryde	1990: Wightlink.
Our Lady Patricia	International Catamarans, Hobart, Australia.	1986	312	-	470	Portsmouth-Ryde	1990: Wightlink.
Lymington	Wm. Denny & Bros Ltd., Dumbarton, U.K.	1938	275	16	400	Lymington-Yarmouth	Withdrawn in 1973. Sold Western Ferries in 1974, renamed **Sound of Sanda**. Withdrawn 1989. Resold for workboat use in 1994.
Farringford	Wm. Denny & Bros Ltd., Dumbarton, U.K.	1947	489	32	800	Lymington-Yarmouth Hull-New Holland	Withdrawn in 1981. Sold to Western Ferries in 1981. Broken up in 1984.
Freshwater	Ailsa Shipbuilding Co. Ltd, Troon, UK.	1959	363	26	620	Lymington-Yarmouth	Withdrawn from service 1985. Sold Western Ferries 1986, renamed **Sound of Seil**. Resold for use as crane barge in 1996.
Fishbourne	Philip & Son Ltd, Dartmouth, UK.	1961	293	34	168	Portsmouth-Fishbourne	Withdrawn from service 1983. Sold for scrap, resold Cyprus 1984 renamed **Kibris I.** Lost in 1985.
Camber Queen	Philip & Son Ltd, Dartmouth, UK.	1961	293	34	168	Portsmouth-Fishbourne	Withdrawn 1983. Sold to Portugal in 1984, renamed **Mira Troia**.
Caedmon	Robb Caledon Shipbuilders, Dundee, UK.	1973	764	76	756	Portsmouth-Fishbourne Lymington-Yarmouth	1990: Wightlink.
Cenred	Robb Caledon Shipbuilders, Dundee, UK.	1973	761	76	756	Lymington-Yarmouth	1990: Wightlink.
Cenwulf	Robb Caledon Shipbuilders, Dundee, UK.	1973	761	76	756	Lymington-Yarmouth	1990: Wightlink.
Cuthred	Richards Shipbuilders, Lowestoft, UK.	1969	794	48	745	Portsmouth-Fishbourne	Withdrawn in 1986. Sold for Tyne cruises. 1988 resold Portugal. 1989 renamed **Mira Praia**.
St Catherine	Henry Robb, Leith, UK.	1983	2,036	142	1,000	Portsmouth-Fishbourne	1990: Wightlink.
St. Helen	Henry Robb, Leith, UK.	1983	2,983	142	1,000	Portsmouth-Fishbourne	1990: Wightlink.
St. Cecilia	Cochrane Shipbuilders, Selby, UK.	1987	2,983	142	1,000	Portsmouth-Fishbourne	1990: Wightlink.

Name	Builder	Year	Gross tonnage	Freight/car capacity	Passengers	Sealink route	Other information
St. Faith	Cochrane Shipbuilders, Selby, UK.	1990	2,968	142	1,000	Portsmouth-Fishbourne	1990: Wightlink.

SOUTH WEST – PORTSMOUTH & WEYMOUTH

Name	Builder	Year	Gross tonnage	Freight/car capacity	Passengers	Sealink route	Other information
Caesarea	J.S. White & Co. Ltd, Cowes, UK.	1960	4,174	-	1,400	Weymouth-Channel Islands Folkestone/Dover-Boulogne/Calais	Withdrawn from service 1980. Sold to Hong Hong and renamed **Aesarea**. , then to Philippines, then Japan. Broken up South Korea in 1986
Sarnia	J.S. White & Co. Ltd, Cowes, UK.	1961	4,174	-	1,400	Weymouth-Channel Islands	Withdrawn from service 1977. Sold and renamed **Aquamart**. 1979 sold Saudi Arabia renamed **Golden Star** then **Saudi Golden Star**. Broken up 1987.
Earl Godwin	Oresundsvaret A/B, Landskrona, Norway.	1966	3,999	174	1.050	Weymouth-Channel Islands Weymouth-Cherbourg	ex **Svea Drott**. Purchased by Sealink in 1974. Withdrawn from service 1990. Sold to Italy and renamed **Moby Baby**.
Earl William	Kaldnes Mek Verksted A/S, Tonsberg, Norway.	1964	3,984	140	600	Portsmouth/Weymouth-Channel Islands Liverpool-Dun Laoghaire	ex. **Viking II**. Purchased by Sealink in 1976. Withdrawn from service 1992. Sold to Greece and renamed **Pearl William**.
Earl Granville	Jos L. Meyer, Papenburg, Germany.	1973	4,477	265	1,200	Potrsmouth/Weymouth-Channel Islands	ex **Viking 4**. Purchased by Sealink in 1981.Withdrawn from service 1990. Sold to Greece and renamed **Express Olympia**.
Earl Harold	Cantieri Navale Breda, Venice, Italy.	1971	3,715	190	1,200	Stranraer-Larne Portsmouth/Weymouth-Channel Islands	ex **Ailsa Princess**. Renamed **Earl Harold** in 1984.Withdrawn from service 1989. Sold to Greece and renamed **Dimitra**. Later renamed **Naias Express**.

FISHGUARD

Name	Builder	Year	Gross tonnage	Freight/car capacity	Passengers	Sealink route	Other information
St. David	Cammell Laird & Co, Birkenhead, UK.	1947	3,783	50	1,300	Fishguard-Rosslare	Converted to side loader. Sold to Greece in 1970. Renamed **Holyhead**. 1979: Broken up.
St. Brendan	Rickmers Werft, Bremerhaven, Germany.	1974	5,443	470	1,084	Fishguard-Rosslare	ex **Stena Normandica**. Renamed **St. Brendan** and purchased by Sealink in 1985. Sold in 1990 to Italy and renamed **Moby Vincent**
Stena Felicity	Oresundsvaret AB, Sweden.	1980	15,000	517	1,832	Fishguard-Rosslare	ex **Visby**. ex **Felicity**

HOLYHEAD

Name	Builder	Year	Gross tonnage	Freight/car capacity	Passengers	Sealink route	Other information
Duke of Rothesay	Wm. Denny & Bros. Ltd, Dumbarton, UK.	1956	4,138	111	1,400	Fishguard-Rosslare	Converted to car ferry. Withdrawn from service 1974. Sold for scrap Scotland in 1975.
Hibernia	Harland & Wolff Ltd, Belfast, UK.	1949	5,284	-	2,255	Holyhead-Dun Laoghaire	Withdrawn from service 1976. Sold Greece and renamed **Express Apollon**. Sold for scrap in India in 1981.
Cambria	Harland & Wolff Ltd, Belfast, UK.	1949	5,284	-	2,255	Holyhead-Dun Laoghaire	Withdrawn from service 1975. Sold in 1976 to Saudi Arabia and renamed **Altaif**. Laid up1978. Foundered Suez Roads in January 1981.
Stena Hibernia	Aalborg Vaerft A/S, Denmark	1976	7,836	336	2,200	Holyhead-Dun Laoghaire	ex **St. Columba**. 1996: renamed **Stena Adventurer**
Stena Cambria	Harland & Wolff Ltd, Belfast, UK.	1979	7,405	309	1,400	Dover-Calais Folkestone-Boulogne Holyhead-Dun Laoghaire	ex **St. Anselm**.
St. Cybi	Verolm Shipbuilders, Cork, Ireland.	1975	2,495	432 metres	12	Holyhead-Dun Laoghaire Fishguard-Rosslare Stranraer-Larne	ex **Dundalk**, ex **Stena Sailer** Withdrawn from service 1990. Sold Greece in 1992 and renamed **Theseus** and converted to passenger ship.

PASSENGER/VEHICLE/RO-RO FREIGHT VESSELS IN REGULAR SERVICE (EXCLUDING SHORT TERM CHARTERS AND CARGO VESSELS) 1970-1995

Name	Builder	Year	Gross tonnage	Freight/car capacity	Passengers	Sealink route	Other information
HEYSHAM							
Duke of Argyll	Harland & Wolff Ltd, Belfast, UK.	1956	4,797	!05	1,400*	Heysham-Belfast	Converted to car ferry. Withdrawn from service in 1975. Sold to Greece in 1975 and renamed **Neptunia**. 1987: **Corinthia**. 1993: **Faith Power**. 1994: **Fairy Princess**. 1994: **Zenith**. Burnt out Hong Kong in August 1995.
Duke of Lancaster	Harland & Wolff Ltd, Belfast, UK.	1956	4,797	105	!,400*	Heysham-Belfast Fishguard-Rosslare Holyhead-Dun Laoghaire	Converted to car ferry. Withdrawn from service 1978. Sold for static use in North Wales.
Manx Viking	S.A. Juliana Construction, Gijon, Spain.	1976	3,589	220	777	Heysham-Douglas	ex **Monte Castillo**. Withdrawn from service 1986. Sold Norway and renamed **Skudenes**. Sold Canada in 1989 and renamed **Nindawayama**.
LAKE DISTRICT							
Tern	Forrest, Wyvenhoe, UK	1891	120		633	Cruises on Lake Windermere	Ownership of vessel transferred to SeaCo in 1985. Sold to local operator in 1993.
Swift	Seath, Rutherglen, UK	1900	203		781	Cruises on Lake Windermere	Ownership of vessel transferred to SeaCo in 1985. Sold to local operator in 1993. Laid up 1982.
Teal	Vickers, Barrow, UK	1936	251		877	Cruises on Lake Windermere	Ownership of vessel transferred to SeaCo in 1985. Sold to local operator in 1993.
Swan	Vickers, Barrow, UK	1938	251		855	Cruises on Lake Windermere	Ownership of vessel transferred to SeaCo in 1985. Sold to local operator in 1993.
STRANRAER							
Caledonian Princess	Wm. Denny & Bros. Ltd, Belfast, UK.	1961	3,630	103*	1,400*	Stranraer-Larne, Fishguard-Rosslare, Weymouth-Channel Islands & Dover-Boulogne/Calais	Withdrawn from service 1981. Sold and renamed **Tuxedo Princess** for night club use on the Tyne and then Clyde.
Antrim Princess	Hawthorn Leslie, Hebburn, Tyne, UK.	1967	3,762	170	1,200	Stranraer-Larne	1985: Renamed **Tynwald**. Withdrawn from service 1990. Sold to Italy and renamed **Lauro Express**.
Darnia	Oosterreichische Schiffswerften AG, Linz Kornenburg, Austria.	1976	3,455	740 trailer metres	400	Stranraer-Larne	ex **Stena Topper** Withdrawn from service 1991. Sold and renamed **Nord Neptunus**.
Ulidia	Kristiansand M/V, A/S. Kristiansand, Norway.	1970	1,599	540 lane metres	20	Irish sea freight services.	ex **Stena Carrier**. Withdrawn from service 1981. Sold and renamed **Auto Trader**, then 1986: **Raga Queen**. 1988: **Fjordveien**. 1994: **Fjardvagen**. 1995: **Holgerstjern**.
Dalriada	Brodrena Lothe A/S, Haugesund, Norway.	1971	1,600	540 lane metres	12	Irish Sea freight services	ex **Stena Trailer**. On charter from Stena Line. 1980: **Viking Trader**. 1981: **Stena Trader**. 1985: **Trader** 1986: **Trailer**. 1992: **Sarmacja**.
Anderida	Trosvik Verksted A/S, Brevik, Norway.	1972	1,600	540 lane metres	12	Dover-Dunkerque & Irish Sea freight services.	Withdrawn from service 1981. Sold Greece and renamed **Truck Trader**, renamed Sealink (New Zealand), **Mirela** then **CTMA Voyageur** (Canada).
Stena Antrim	Harland & Wolff, Belfast, UK.	1980	7,399	309	1,400	Dover-Calais Stranraer-Larne	ex **St. Christopher**.
Stena Caledonia	Harland & Wolff, Belfast, UK.	1981	7,196	309	1000	Stranraer-Larne Holyhead-Dun Laoghaire Dover-Ostend	ex **St David**.
Stena Galloway	Harland & Wolff, Belfast, UK.	1979	6,630	309	1,200	Stranraer-Larne	ex **Galloway Princess**

Name	Builder	Year	Gross tonnage	Freight/car capacity	Passengers	Sealink route	Other information
HUMBER							
Tattershall Castle	Wm. Grey & Co Ltd, West Harttlepool, UK.	1934	556	20	940	Hull-New Holland	Withdrawn 1972. In static use on the Rover Thames.
Wingfield Castle	Wm. Grey & Co Ltd, West Harttlepool, UK.	1934	556	20	940	Hull-New Holland	Withdrawn 1974. In static useat West Hartlepool.
Lincoln Castle	A&J Inglis Ltd., Glasgow, U.K.	1940	598	20	940	Hull-New Holland	Withdrown 1978. In static use at Grimsby Heritage Centre.
OTHER SERVICES							
Orient Express	Dubigenon Normandie, Nantes, France.	1975	12,343	240	791	Mediterranean service from Venice.	ex **Bore Star**. ex **Silja Star**.

*Weymouth October 1971 - Left to right, the **Sarnia**, **Maid of Kent** and **Caledonian Princess**. (Jim Ashby)*

SEALINK OPERATING PARTNERS

R.M.T. (until 1985)

Koning Albert	1947-78
Prince Philippe (II)	1948-73
Car Ferry/Prinses Josephine Charlotte (II)	1949-76
Roi Leopold III	1956-78
Koningin Elizabeth	1957-78
Reine Astrid (I)	1958-82
Artevelde	1958-76
Koningin Fabiola	1962-85
Roi Baudouin	1965-83
Prinses Paola	1966-87
Princesse Astrid (II)	1968-83
Prins Philippe (III)	1973-86
Prince Laurent	1974-92
Prinses Maria-Esmeralda	1975-95
Princesse Marie-Christine	1976
Prins Albert (III)	1978
Princesse Clementine (II) (Jetfoil)	1981
Prinses Stephanie (Jetfoil)	1981
Stena Nautica/Reine Astrid (II)	1975-1982

*The **Valencay** arriving at Dieppe. (Miles Cowsill)*

S.M.Z. (until 1991)

Koningin Wilhelmina	1960-79
Koningin Juliana	1968-84
Prinses Beatrix	1978-85
Koningin Beatrix	1986

S.N.C.F. (until 1995)

SEALINK FERRIES SNCF

Saint-Germain	1951-88
Transcontainer I	1969-86
Capitaine Le Goff	1972-81
Nord Pas-de-Calais	1987
Cote d'Azur (II)	1951-72
Compiegne	1958-81
Villandry	1965-84
Valencay	1965-84
Chantilly	1966-87
Chartres	1974-93
Cote d'Azur (III)	1980
Fiesta	1990

*The final R.M.T. passenger vessel **Prinses Paola** arriving at Dover in September 1985. (John Hendy)*